FAMILY SECRETS

Other Books in the Minirth Meier New Life Clinic Series

For general information about Minirth Meier New Life Clinic branch offices, counseling services, educational resources, and hospital programs, call toll free 1-800-NEW-LIFE.

FAMILY SECRETS

Michael Mask

Julie L. Mask

Jeanne Hensley

Steven L. Craig

THOMAS NELSON PUBLISHERS

Nashville • Atlanta • London • Vancouver

Published in Nashville, Tennessee, by Thomas Nelson, Inc., Publishers, and distributed in Canada by Word Communications, Ltd., Richmond, British Columbia.

The Bible version used in this publication is THE NEW KING JAMES VERSION. Copyright © 1979, 1980, 1982, 1990, Thomas Nelson, Inc., Publishers.

ISBN 0-7852-8322-6

Printed in the United States of America.

Contents

Acknowledgments

We would like to express our appreciation to Kay Strom, who transformed our notes, tapes, thoughts, and transcripts into a readable form with such skill, and to Janet Thoma and her staff at Thomas Nelson Publishers, whose support and editorial expertise were invaluable.

Michael and Julie would like to thank Dr. Frank Minirth, Dr. Paul Meier, and Janet Thoma for giving them the opportunity to share their thoughts in print. They would also like to thank their parents, Juanita, Bill, Anna, and Frankie, for their continual support.

Jeanne would like to thank her family, including her sons, Tim and Steve Smith, who put up with a crazy schedule and take-out meals and told her to "hang in there" anyway; her parents, Debs and Ethel Hensley; and her sister, Debbie Rush, whose encouragement and support have meant so much. Thanks to close friends Kay Newton, Pat and Jim Mickler, and Eileen and Dennis Troup for helping in so many ways during the frequent writing trips to San Antonio, as well as to Uncle

Harry Meadows and Cousin Donna Woods for the wonderful hospitality and accommodations. Invaluable professional advice and insight has come from Dr. Kay Nelson and Dr. Mary Lou Holt of Texas A & M University, Corpus Christi; Bea Hammonds, Director of Lutheran Social Service in Corpus Christi; and Don Kinner of The Center for Christian Family Counseling.

Steven would like to thank Michael and Julie Mask for allowing him to be a part of this important and much-needed book. His hope is that his contributions in some small way help fulfill their expectations and desires. He would also like to thank his wife, Jan, and their six children, Jason, Megan, Josh, Morgan, Mallory, and Zach, for their sacrifices and patience. If he had it to do over again, he would probably do some things differently. However, by God's grace, they have all persevered and endured.

1

The Cost
of Keeping
the Secret

Laura Thompson, a tall, thin teenager with dark curly hair and green eyes, had been going through what her parents called "a rebellious stage." She had always had lots of friends and her grades had always been good, but now there were complaints from school about her cutting classes and, in the principal's words, "generally mouthing off." At home she was increasingly sullen and withdrawn.

Then the unthinkable happened: Laura told her mom and dad that she was pregnant. Laura's parents decided it would be in everyone's best interest to keep her condition a secret, so they sent Laura out West to live with Aunt Jenny. "Just a little time away to help her make a break from those friends of hers who are such a bad influence," they explained to their family and friends. "She'll have a great senior year out there in California. She is going to try out for the cheerleading squad, you know."

Secret-keeping was nothing new to Jim and Betty Thompson. They themselves had had to get married because Betty was pregnant with Laura. Jim's parents were respectable professional people who seldom talked about anything personal. His father was a cold, critical perfectionist; his mother a homemaker whose main concern was keeping everyone happy. Betty's parents were upright and religious, but their view of God was one of wrath and punishment tempered with very little love and mercy. Both families had insisted that Jim and Betty get married immediately and lock their shameful secret away. Certainly they had never talked about it to Laura and her sister, Bonnie, as the girls were growing up.

No one, not even Bonnie, was told about the baby girl Laura delivered and immediately put up for adoption. Yet Bonnie knew that something had happened. "I think Laura had an abortion," she whispered to her best friend.

"That would be the *worst*," her friend said. "Laura would never do that, would she?"

"Only if my parents *made* her do it," Bonnie said.

The more Bonnie thought about it, the more certain she became that this was exactly what had happened. And the more certain she became, the angrier she grew. "I hate my parents!" she wrote in her diary.

When Laura came back home, no one talked about her school year with Aunt Jennie. Although everyone valiantly pretended that nothing was wrong, the tension in the Thompson house was thick and heavy. As the months passed, Bonnie felt more and more isolated from the rest of her family, even though she hadn't done anything wrong. And all the time her anger at her parents grew and seethed and grew some more.

Laura tried to smooth things out with Bonnie; she really did. But whenever she attempted to reach out to her sister, she felt like she was talking to a door that had been slammed shut and bolted tight. Although Bonnie never said so, she made it obvious that she wanted nothing to do with Laura.

Bonnie was also carefully watching the change that was taking place in her parents. Increasingly her father withdrew from the family and took refuge at work. Her mother was drinking more and more. "It's because they are feeling guilty about what they made Laura do," Bonnie told herself.

Then one Saturday night at dinner, the truth about Laura's pregnancy and the baby's adoption came tumbling out.

"Why didn't anyone tell me?" Bonnie demanded.

"It was better you didn't know," her father insisted. "We didn't want to get you involved."

Was it better to keep the secret?

After watching the terrible pain her sister had put her parents through, as well as feeling guilty about her own accusing feelings toward them, Bonnie promised herself, "I'll never add to their hurt." And so she set about attempting to remake herself into a perfect daughter. The price was isolation and depression as she bent all her efforts toward achieving and succeeding.

Did Laura's rebellion destroy her family? No. Was

it her pregnancy? It was not. The damage was done by the keeping of the secret.

Anna Karenina, Leo Tolstoy's great tragic novel, begins this way: "Happy families are all alike; every unhappy family is unhappy in its own way." Perhaps so, yet the majority of unhappy families are alike in one important way—almost all of them harbor family secrets.

God uniquely designed the family to provide for the welfare of children: to train them, to love them, to rear them in such a way that when they become adults they will in turn be able to provide adequately for themselves and their own families. In healthy families there is a quality of realness. A trust is established, and parents can be relied upon and believed. There is an expectation that "what you see is what you get." In unhealthy families, that realness is missing. The family harbors anger, low self-esteem, and shame, yet the family message insists, "We're okay! Certainly we are better than most families."

To put things in their proper perspective, the only perfectly functional families are Beaver Cleaver's family and the Brady Bunch. Unfortunately, unlike life in television land, real-life problems can't be fixed in thirty minutes minus commercial breaks. Such fantasy families are called "suprafunctional" because they represent perfection far beyond what is possible for normal families. The only suprafunctional relationship is the one we experience through our relationship with God.

All families face tragedies. All families suffer pain and loss. How we handle the situations that life thrusts upon us determine the course our lives will take. If we choose to face tragedy with courage, honesty, and a willingness to let God change us, we will be strengthened and made more Christlike. But if we choose to be secretive, to cover up and push aside the pain that comes with the difficult situations of life, the result will be bitterness, anger, depression, and ultimately, dysfunction for ourselves and our families.

Functional or Dysfunctional?

We hear a lot today about functional families and dysfunctional families, with a variety of definitions. For clarity here, we will define *functional families* as those in which each family member's needs are adequately met most of the time. Although functional means healthy, it does not mean perfect. Problems arise, but when they do, they are handled in ways that build relationships within the family. In *dysfunctional families,* on the other hand, emotional needs are *not* met. (See figure 1.1.) These unmet needs cause so much harm to the members of the family that they are not able to develop to their full potential.

Even functional families have a few skeletons stuffed in the back of their closets. Perhaps there is a bankruptcy they don't talk about, an alcoholic uncle whose "problem" is never discussed, a pregnancy before marriage that is never admitted, a painful loss that

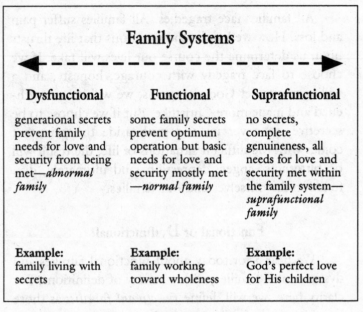

Family Systems

Dysfunctional	Functional	Suprafunctional
generational secrets prevent family needs for love and security from being met—*abnormal family*	some family secrets prevent optimum operation but basic needs for love and security mostly met —*normal family*	no secrets, complete genuineness, all needs for love and security met within the family system—*suprafunctional family*
Example: family living with secrets	**Example:** family working toward wholeness	**Example:** God's perfect love for His children

Figure 1.1

is not acknowledged, or a family member's affair everyone pretends not to know about. Even so, the members of the family—including the secret-keepers—remain basically functional. Why is this so? Because functional families, even though they are far from flawless, are able to meet many of the members' basic needs for acceptance, love, and security. Although the families do have their problems and the family members don't always function perfectly—they get irritated, they yell at their kids, sometimes they get divorced, and they do many things they are ashamed of—they still manage to hang in there.

Sound like any family you know? Probably so. That's exactly where many of us are.

Secret Keeping Is Nothing New

A man after God's own heart—what a wonderful way to be recorded in the annals of history. Yet King David had his family troubles—and his secrets. Consider the account in Second Samuel 11 where we read that David saw another man's wife, and oh, how he wanted her! Since he was the king of Israel and could do whatever he wanted, he took her. Lust was to grow into a family problem. In Second Samuel 13:1 we read: "After this Absalom the son of David had a lovely sister, whose name was Tamar; and Amnon the son of David loved her." Where did this incestuous love lead? To disaster. Amnon raped his half sister, and eventually he was killed by Absalom. As for Absalom, he led a rebellion against his father David, and he, too, was killed.

David was a good man, but he made a serious mistake that planted the seeds of tragedy that were later reaped by his children.

Family secrets don't have to be of rape or mayhem or murder to do generational damage. Consider the great patriarch, Abraham. On two different occasions he told two different kings that Sarah was not his wife, but his sister (see Gen. 12, 20). As a matter of fact, Sarah was his half sister as well as his wife, a situation that wasn't considered incestuous in those days. But that wasn't the point. Sarah, you see, was a beautiful woman, and her husband Abraham was afraid he would be killed because of her. So he decided to lie his way out of the situation. Each time, when the deception was revealed, the king released Sarah to Abraham and away they went. There seemed to be no consequences other than a stern rebuke from the king involved. But the matter didn't end there.

True to family tradition, Abraham's son Isaac lied to the Philistine king, telling him that Isaac's wife Rebekah was *his* sister (see Gen. 26). Again, no great damage was done. But the family pattern of deception manifested itself yet again in the third generation when Isaac's son Jacob lied to his father and stole his twin brother Esau's birthright and blessing (see Gen. 27). And years later—in the fourth generation—the now established family pattern led Jacob's sons to lie to their father and sell their brother Joseph into Egyptian slavery (see Gen. 37).

Eventually there was healing in the family, but it came only after the secret was exposed in Egypt and forgiveness followed (see Gen. 42–47).

Secrets hurt. They cause loneliness and guilt and rejection and fear and anger. No matter how deeply they are buried or how carefully they are tucked away, our family secrets invariably reappear in our children and in our children's children. And each time they reappear, the toll they exact is higher and more painful.

Dynamics of Family Secrets

"But," you may be saying, "surely there are matters that should be kept private." Of course there are. What sets a family secret apart from a matter that is appropriately kept confidential within the family is the effect it has on that family. Confidentiality protects and strengthens the family; secrets damage the family. Although a secret has power over the family, the family doesn't talk about it. A confidential matter shouldn't be discussed in the neighborhood or at church or in the workplace, but the family can be open about it among themselves, and they can strive together to work out any problems it presents. Even intimately private issues that are just between a husband and wife can be discussed openly between them.

There is also a difference between a secret and a surprise. We keep surprises for a while, then we share them (surprise parties, for instance, or the fact that Mom is pregnant or that Dad is changing jobs). Surprises have healthy boundaries, while secrets go on and on and on.

Generally speaking, the more openness there is within a family, the healthier that family will be.

Secrets Tend to Be Generational

"My family has ruined everything," Bonnie Thompson said miserably. "There is no way out for me. My parents are wrecks. My sister is a wreck. I'm a wreck. And if I ever marry and have children, they will all be wrecks, too. Welcome to the family, kids!"

Secrets that are not dealt with do have an almost uncanny way of repeating themselves in the generations to come. It would seem that as the original secret-keepers die, the secrets and their power would die with them. Instead, the secrets are converted into anger, shame, and unresolved pain and then carried on to the next generation where they tend to manifest themselves in different ways.

As we saw in Abraham's family, behaviors that come about as the result of keeping secrets set up patterns that continue from one generation to the next. Scripture warns us of this when it speaks of the sins of the fathers being passed on to the third and fourth generations. These passed-on sins can well be the family patterns that result from secrets: guilt, anxiety, fear, and rage. Unresolved, these emotions wreak havoc in a family, generation after generation after generation.

Family secrets that remain hidden do not go away.

Secrets Grow More Powerful

"Our secret destroyed our family," Jim Thompson told us. "Why didn't we just deal with it back then when it wasn't so big? Why did we have to wait until it caused so much damage?"

Why indeed? When we hide a secret and attempt to cover it, it becomes like a malignant tumor. Quietly, slowly, it grows and grows until it threatens the very health of the family. A small sin, a little lie, a bit of a cover-up, and a secret is born. Unconfronted, that secret grows ever more powerful as it passes from generation to generation.

Secrets Exact a Price

In healthy families, each person is authentic. Mom and Dad and the kids are who they seem to be, both within their families and to the world outside. But in secret-keeping families, this sense of authenticity is lost. What is inside is almost never what people on the outside see.

"No one really cared about me," Laura told us.

"You!" Bonnie retorted. "It was *me* no one cared about! Everyone lied to me!"

"We cared about you both," Betty Thompson insisted. "We were trying to protect you."

Protection and love and concern are not what came through to either girl. What came through were guilt, fear, and anger, and the results were loneliness, hurt, and rejection.

Part of *the power of secrets is in the lies that generate them, feed them, and keep them alive.* Living with a secret means remaining entangled in a web of deception. Family members are angry, yet they deny the anger. They are ashamed, yet they insist there is no shame. "Our family is happy," they say. "All families have their problems. This isn't that big a deal."

Deception is so destructive because it breaks trust

and breeds confusion. When emotions are continuously denied and repressed, defense mechanisms rise up to take their place. When children are told, "Don't think, don't see, don't tell, don't feel," they lose their ability to trust.

"You never really loved me," Laura told her parents.

"We did!" they protested. "We *always* loved you!"

The truth was that the Thompsons *did* love Laura, and they loved Bonnie, too. They loved them as well as they could. But the fact was that the girls *felt* unloved, and their feelings seriously undermined their self-worth. They didn't believe they were accepted by the people they needed most.

In healthy families, parents and children recognize their idiosyncrasies and faults. Often they learn to laugh at themselves. Sometimes they even change their behavior. In functional families it's okay not to be perfectly okay. But in less healthy families, the imperative becomes to project a facade of "okay-ness." Like actors playing their roles, parents live behind masks, revealing only what they want others to see. As children watch their parents playing their roles behind those masks, they become increasingly entangled in the secret-keeping. They grow up never really knowing their parents, yet they learn thoroughly to mimic their patterns of behavior.

For families living with secrets, the loneliness can be terribly isolating, especially if they consider their secret disgraceful. They are convinced that if anyone were to discover who they really are and what has happened, they would be rejected outright. Here, then, is one of the heaviest tolls exacted on everyone involved in keeping the secret: They build formidable walls around themselves, and they guard those walls as though their lives depended upon it. They are isolated by their fear that the truth would destroy them.

This is the paradox of family secrets: *What people fear the most—exposing the secret—is the one thing that can bring them healing.* To those outside the family, it may seem obvious. "Why not just tell?" they ask. But those within the system have been reared with the unspoken rule: In order to keep the peace and preserve the family, the secret must not be told. To tell would be to betray the family and ruin us all.

Secret-keeping families are based on guilt and shame. Repressed under the family mythology that "We are happy" is the tough reality of deep unhappiness.

"Why can't our family be like everybody else's?" Bonnie asked. "What is wrong with us?"

Feeling different and guilty and ashamed, secret-keeping families grow increasingly angry. The downward spiral is relentless. Secrets lead to isolation, shame, and worthlessness, which lead to anger and guilt, which feed the fear, which keeps the secret alive.

Hopeless? Not at all.

The Cycle Can Be Broken

"Why didn't anyone tell me what was going on?" Bonnie demanded of her family.

That's a good question. The answer is both simple and complex. Family members don't talk about the family secret because they are afraid they will be rejected and end up isolated and lonely. Or they are afraid everyone will point at them and say, "It's all your fault!" They are paralyzed by fear.

Bonnie worries a lot about the next generation. "I have a serious boyfriend," she told us. "Someday I want to marry him. But what about our children? Will they be messed up like my sister and me?"

Bonnie, like most people, understands that family problems are passed on from one generation to the next. Families cannot change the past. What happened in the family, happened. Nothing that was done can be undone. But the future is by no means sealed. The secret can be revealed, and healing can begin.

It is the secret that perpetuates the action and the lies of family problems. Children raised by abusive parents tend to be abusive because they didn't talk about the abuse or get help in handling it. Parents who take financial liberties raise children who are likely to cheat on their taxes or even defraud their companies because the silence seems to say that it is acceptable behavior.

But it doesn't matter how mild or how heinous the secret—abuse, lies, addiction, incest. Whatever happened, a family does not have to be doomed by the past. Right now, in this generation, the secret can be stopped and the pattern of pain broken.

Speaking out is well worth the effort. Keeping a family secret takes a great deal of energy. Freed of that burden, the families' energy can go into loving each other and building each other up. And that is a solid base for hope. Secrets break down communication and keep families from knowing who they really are. When family members share secret sins and past failures with each other, they are being real and communicating their vulnerability. That vulnerability in relationships is the source of strength. To be real and vulnerable and honest, to let those close to us see us as we really are, to experience their love and acceptance—this is to be whole, healed, and at peace.

Where Are You?

When do families cross over the line between functional and dysfunctional when it comes to family secrets? To evaluate the situation in your own family, answer the following twenty questions, marking yes or no beside each one.

FAMILY SECRETS INVENTORY

Yes   *No*

____ ____   1. Does someone in your family keep "little secrets" or tell "little white lies?"

____ ____   2. Is there a certain topic (or topics) that is never discussed (money, sex, etc.)?

Yes	No	
___	___	3. Are there certain members of your family no one talks about?
___	___	4. Does anyone in your family lie about the cost of something?
___	___	5. Is there some past incident in your family that no one talks about?
___	___	6. Are you unable to share emotions freely and honestly with your siblings and parents, feeling a need to "be strong" or "be quiet" even when you are hurting?
___	___	7. Is there one member of your family through whom everyone else filters information in order to keep another family member in the dark ("Let's not tell Dad; it will only upset him")?
___	___	8. Have you ever suspected or discovered unexpectedly that someone in your family was unfaithful to his or her spouse?
___	___	9. Has anyone in your family ever said, "Don't tell anyone about this"?
___	___	10. Is there an unspoken message given that family business is not to be discussed outside your home?
___	___	11. Are there any long-term feuds or grudges between members of your family?
___	___	12. Is your family structured in such a way that one person or group of people are so powerful that the less powerful members keep silent to protect themselves?
___	___	13. Is anyone in your family "explosive" or does anyone have a temper that is considered a normal family trait?

Yes *No*

____ ____ 14. Is it unacceptable to discuss the death of a family member openly?

____ ____ 15. Is it unacceptable to express appropriate anger within your family system?

____ ____ 16. Is it forbidden to feel "negative" emotions such as crying, sadness, or distress within your family?

____ ____ 17. Is someone in your family afraid of another family member?

____ ____ 18. When you lived at home, did you feel it wasn't safe to bring friends home?

____ ____ 19. Does anyone in your family have an addictive behavior (involving, for instance, drugs, alcohol, food, gambling, credit cards, or work) that is never talked about?

____ ____ 20. Do your parents argue frequently, yet no one talks about it?

Now count the number of marks in the yes column. If you have:

0–5   Congratulations! Your family is in good shape.

6–10   Your family probably works well most of the time, but there are some secrets that need to be addressed.

11–15   Your family has lots of secrets. This is the time to start dealing with them.

16–20   In addition to reading this book, your family needs to seek professional counseling immediately.

Being able to see where changes are needed in a family is usually not easy. This book addresses the most

common areas of secrets. Reading through these stories of the secrets other families are wrestling with, you
will probably see a lot of people you know—friends,
relatives, coworkers. Now and then you may even catch
a glimpse of yourself. We hope that through this recognition you may learn strategies for discovering your
own secrets, for meeting them head on, and for exposing them. It is this process that will lead you—and perhaps your family as well—to healing.

2

Why the Secrets?

Considering the cost, why do families keep secrets? Why not simply cry out, "Enough, already!" and let them go?

For some families, secret-keeping is the pattern of their life, and it takes a great deal of courage to break out from the familiar pattern to the unknown of new behaviors. Others find their sense of success and competence so tied to the keeping of the secret that to break its power would be tantamount to destroying themselves. Still other secret-keepers sincerely believe that by keeping quiet they are protecting others in the family.

One sixteen-year-old high school student found her whole life upside down when she came across an old letter. The correspondence revealed that the woman she had always thought was her mother was in fact her grandmother. Her older brothers and sisters were really her aunts and uncles—except her sister Maureen, who, it turned out, was really her mother. For seventeen years the family had conspired to keep the secret to protect her. But her reaction? "Something must be terribly wrong with me, or my entire family wouldn't have lied to me my whole life."

Many secrets are kept out of fear ("What would happen to us if people knew?"), while others are kept out of pride ("How could we ever face our friends?"). Some people realize something should be done, but they are just not sure what that something is.

"My mother wanted to stop the secrets in my own family," says one young woman, "but she didn't know how. She thought it was enough to simply tell me, 'Staying in a relationship that makes you unhappy is bad. That's what I did all my life. Don't you do it.'"

Why Are Secrets Kept?

Secrets Are Kept Because People Feel Ashamed and Guilty

Shame and guilt (whether true guilt or false) are among the most common causes of secret-keeping.

Guilt: True or false?

True guilt comes from God. When He shows us our faults, He lets us know exactly what we are guilty of doing, what we should be doing instead, and how we can rectify what we have done wrong.

Here is an example. A parent lashes out in anger at her son whose room, as usual, is a complete mess. "You're lazy!" she yells. "You never do anything I ask you to do! You are always messing up!" The next day, after cooling off, she feels guilty for the verbal attack. She knows what she needs to do: Apologize and ask his forgiveness for attacking him, tell him that she loves him, and explain that messy rooms disturb her and that she needs his cooperation in keeping his room acceptable. The secret is *Mom has a bad temper*.

True guilt isn't bad. If we respond to it appropriately, it will take us a long way toward restoring broken relationships, and we will grow in the process.

False guilt is an entirely different matter. It comes from not meeting a set of false expectations or standards, from feeling we are "not good enough." It wistfully mourns what could have been. Vague and built on lies and half-truths, false guilt destroys relationships and stands in the way of spiritual growth.

Reviewing the messy room incident, the voice of false guilt would accuse, "You are a totally worthless parent! You yell at your son, and he won't even listen to you. Why, you can't even get him to clean his room! Just listen to the way you talked to him. And you call yourself a Christian!"

See the difference? God uses true guilt to restore our relationships with Him and with others. But false guilt damages relationships, fosters secrets, and gives them power. False guilt isn't a secret itself, but it can give one a sense that *I am bad* and *I need to hide this*.

While true guilt comes from God, false guilt comes from our past, our own expectations, or from the people around us. The Pharisees were especially adept at piling on false guilt. They loaded the law onto God's people and then condemned them when they couldn't obey every jot and tittle. There are people like that today in all aspects of our lives—our jobs, our families, our churches. They set rules and regulations, stress legalism, and are quick to judge anyone who breaks their rules—often in an effort to hide their own faults.

Shame

Although Ross had been a straight-A student, he seldom heard words of praise from his family. What he did hear was, "You could do better if you really tried. You should be the best in your class." Long before he knew anything about the term *conditional love,* he was well aware that approval was based on what he did rather than on who he was. If it wasn't perfection, it was shameful. The secret in Ross's family is *You're only accepted if you're perfect.*

Ross's father had been raised by parents who pointed out every fault and mistake their son made, but let his strengths and successes pass unmentioned. When he grew up he was determined to be a good dad to his own son, so he parented Ross the only way he knew how, with criticism and shame for anything he saw as a failure.

Now Ross is grown and has a son of his own who he hardly ever criticizes. Why? Because Ross, in an effort to prove himself, has become such a workaholic that he rarely sees his son.

The messages of shame that families pass on sharpen and preserve their secrets. Shame in itself may or may not be kept secret, but it is a driving force that works as a tool to draw people into hiding their pain. Shame messages include such pronouncements as:

- "You should be ashamed of yourself."
- "A good Christian wouldn't do such a thing."
- "You could have done better."
- "You should be the best."

Guilt and shame lead to another major cause of family secrets: the fear of failure.

Secrets Are Kept Because People Fear Failure

Fearing failure is a driving force that tricks people into believing they should keep anything short of success to themselves because of "what people will think." Those who aren't afraid of failure can generally talk about their shortcomings without worry that others may judge or condemn them. People who suffer from a fear of failure tend to have several characteristics in common:

- *They believe they are not as good as others.* Most people who fear failure sincerely believe that other people are better and more competent than they are.

- *They must achieve.* While believing others may be better than themselves, they try to prove their worth by driving themselves to perform well above what other people expect of them.

Teddy is a good example. When he won two races in a district track meet (placing a full minute ahead of the second place runner), he was furious with himself. "I wanted to finish in eight minutes," he lamented, "but it took me eight minutes and ten seconds."

- *They are afraid of letting someone down.* "My dad was counting on me to set a new record," Teddy said of his performance at the track meet. "Now I've let him down."

- *They see love and acceptance as being tied to achievement.* When asked how he thought his father felt about him, Teddy said, "I'm sure he loves me, but I don't think he is very proud of me."

- *They may set their standards too low and only attempt what they are good at.* They don't dare challenge themselves. If they did, how could they be sure they wouldn't fail?

- *They may set standards for themselves that are unattainable.* This is not the same as presenting themselves with a challenge. People who fear failure are so perfectionistic that they may doom themselves to fail before they even begin.

"Every one of these characteristics describes me," admits one wife. "My position in the family was that of peacemaker. I was a pleaser. I thought it was my job to keep peace. When I married my husband, my perfectionism fit right into his mold of expectations. I figured if I could do everything right, he wouldn't ever get angry at me."

Families pass on messages of failure, too; messages such as:

- "In our family, we don't fail."
- "We don't quit and we never give up!"
- "If you can't do it right, don't do it at all."
- "This is okay, but it would be even better if. . . ."
- "What will everyone think?"
- "If it's not right, it's not *my* fault!"

"If you can't do it right, don't do it at all. That was our family's motto," Gwen said. So what did she do? She seldom tried anything. "It's sad," she noted, "because some of the things I passed up, I later found I was pretty good at. Not great, but good enough to have had fun participating."

That wasn't Alan's problem. Throughout junior and senior high school, he played on the basketball team. "I hated it," he said bitterly. "I was the worst player on the team. Most games I just sat on the bench." So why did he play? "Because my dad wanted me to. It was so important to him that I just couldn't let him down."

Many of us were led to fear failing by the messages we were given by well-meaning moms and dads: *We would love you more if we could be proud of you.*

Secrets Are Kept Because People Want to Escape Reality

After Roger's father deserted his family for another woman, Roger vowed he would never cause his family such pain. When he married, he would be a loving husband and father.

Nine years later, after four years of a happy marriage, Roger's wife gave birth to a son who suffered from a serious heart defect that doctors warned would certainly be fatal. Roger couldn't bear to see his child suffer, and he couldn't bring himself to get close to the boy he was sure to lose. Instead of sharing his anguish with his wife, who was also hurting terribly, Roger started leaving the office with a group of guys who regularly headed to a local bar for happy hour. Alcohol offered Roger an escape from his painful reality. It also led to the eventual breakup of his marriage.

There are characteristics common to people who approach problems by escaping from reality. This is a form of secret-keeping in which people evade the truth of their lives. These people can be termed "reality escape artists" as they hide from themselves, family, friends, work, school, or whatever is painful.

- *They become addicted.* Because they cannot face the pain of tragedy and death, people who try to escape from reality become addicted to something. Whether drugs or alcohol or sex or overeating, addiction is an ever present possibility.

- *They cannot take responsibility.* Responsibility means reality, and reality is too harsh. That is not for them.

- *They are in denial.* Staying in denial is important to them, because it is through denial that they are attempting to numb their pain.

- *They disengage from those around them.* Remaining emotionally aloof from others allows them to continue to deny reality. They are unwilling to confront anyone or anything, for confrontation requires acknowledging what is real.

- *They bury themselves in busyness.* Staying busy is an effective way of escaping reality. That's why so many become workaholics.

"I never can get anything settled with my husband," Carole said in exasperation. "If I even begin to confront him, all of a sudden he's talking about something way off the subject. The other day, he got home really late. I was telling him that he *has* to call me and let me know when he's going to be so late, and out of the blue he said, 'That new tree I planted out front sure is growing well.' "

Carole's husband is a good example of a person who escapes from reality. As he avoids his wife, he keeps his personal thoughts secret. It is as if he thinks, *If I don't have to face my problems, they will go away.* "He's been like this ever since I've known him," Carole says.

Very likely he developed the strategy in childhood.

There are several common family messages that encourage children to grow up being reality escape artists. These include:

- "I don't want to talk about it."
- "If we ignore the problem, it will go away."
- "If we don't talk about it, then the problem doesn't really exist."
- "We will only think happy thoughts."
- "We'll worry about that tomorrow."

The attempt to escape reality is nothing new. The Bible is filled with examples of people who tried this tactic. Jonah is a perfect example. God had a plan for saving Nineveh, but Jonah didn't like it at all. So he simply refused to acknowledge the reality that God will do what He will do. "No problem," Jonah decided. "I'll take a ship in the opposite direction." But reality is reality, whether a person recognizes it or not. God taught Jonah that lesson by means of a three day stay inside a big fish.

Secrets Are Kept Because People Fear Intimacy

Scott, a young surgeon, was quiet, shy, and surprisingly introverted. But his wife desperately longed to be close to him, and she begged him to spend time with her and their young son. Deep down Scott knew she was right, but he couldn't bring himself to be so vulnerable. He escaped the reality of intimacy with his family by working seventy-five hours a week. Scott became a workaholic because his work protected him from having to face his uncomfortable relationships at home.

Fearing intimacy prevents people from getting close and communicating openly, and gives rise to secrecy. People who fear intimacy have several characteristics in common.

- *They fear being rejected, yet they crave love.* If they don't believe they can give loved ones what they need, they are sure the loved ones will turn on them.

- *They suffered hurts in the past.* Whatever the hurt—abuse, neglect, or even "smothering"—they feel betrayed. The result is that they no longer trust intimacy.

- *They believe they are unlovable.* In their minds, intimacy would only let others know how unlovable they are.

- *They have something to hide.* Whether it be negative (such as an affair) or positive (protecting a spouse), a secret keeps others at a distance.

- *They play roles to hide their true selves.* Many people only pretend that they are happy. They tell themselves, "If people really knew me, they wouldn't love me."

- *They have not been able to bond.* Unfortunately, there are many people today who have never bonded with anyone. They have no experience of being loved by another person. When these people become parents, they may totally ignore their children or they may try to show love by showering their kids with material things. But they never give what their children want most—hugs and kisses and emotional involvement. The secret they share is *If people really knew me, they wouldn't like me.*

In the Rivera family, everyone is so afraid of intimacy that they have a television set in every room, and those sets are always on. From the oldest to the youngest, the Riveras are addicted to television. It crowds out any real chance of conversation or sharing. And what if someone needs to talk? The family message comes through loud and clear: "Not now, I'm watching TV."

Although Gabe Rivera doesn't remember it, his father used to listen to the radio just as addictively. It kept him from having to talk to his wife. His grandfather had made a habit of reading the newspaper at the table—that way he didn't have to talk with his family. For generations, the Riveras' family message has been, "Keep your distance from me."

Other negative family messages on intimacy include:

- "We don't talk about feelings."
- "Don't touch me."

- "I'll praise you for what you did, not for who you are."
- "We don't speak of our love for each other."
- "I was just kidding. Can't you take a joke?"
- "If they knew me, they wouldn't like me."

Cynthia was thirty years old when her parents brought her in for counseling. Married just out of high school, Cynthia had soon gotten a divorce and then married again. Two years later her husband committed suicide. She quickly got involved with her boss at work and gave birth to a baby out of wedlock. "She's a mess!" her mother said as they sat down.

"Why?" Cynthia's father demanded of his daughter. "Why do you insist on behaving this way?"

Both parents hammered away relentlessly at their daughter until they were asked, "How often do you tell Cynthia you love her?"

Both parents stared blankly. "Of course we love her," her mother said. "She knows that."

"But how often do you tell her?" pressed the counselor. "How often do you give her hugs?"

"We don't do that kind of thing in our family," her father said.

What was Cynthia's secret? She felt unloved because she had never been told she was loved. Fearing intimacy, yet desperate for it, she jumped from relationship to relationship, looking for love in all the wrong places.

Secrets Are Kept Because People Look for the Easy Way Out

Emily grew up in a loving, male-dominated home with a father who was never confronted by anyone. When she became a mother, Emily did not allow confrontation either. She adamantly insisted to her two children that their father was never to be challenged.

If you were to meet Emily and her children (who are now grown), you would think they are happy. What you wouldn't see is the anger seething beneath the surface that they are handling through addictive behaviors. The son is a workaholic, and the daughter shops compulsively. Both are taking the easiest way out, although their behavior exacts a terribly high cost.

People who look for the easiest way out often find secret-keeping to be easier than disclosing the truth. They share several characteristics:

- They deny.
- They give up.
- They lie.
- They manipulate.
- They avoid conflict at all costs.
- They tell other people what those folks want to hear.
- They are not ones to delay gratification.

What makes people resort to the "easiest way out" approach to life? Their secret is *I'm afraid of confrontation*. One cause is being raised by overly strict parents who never give their children permission to fail. What such parents don't realize is that they actually are encouraging their children to lie their way out of difficult situations. The children are so afraid of their parents' wrath that they don't dare risk telling the truth.

One father was sadly puzzled that none of his children were living a Christlike life. "I just don't get it," he said. "My kids went to church every Sunday, and they listened to the sermons. I know because I quizzed them on the way home."

The kids may have listened, but they didn't apply what they heard to their lives. What they got out of the sermon was nothing more than a list of answers to a quiz. Because their father didn't truly understand love, he was unable to model the love of Christ, and so his children never learned to understand God's love.

Kids also learn to look for the easiest way out when they see their parents operating on that principle— when Mom and Dad lie for their kids, for instance, making excuses for their difficulties. It's also a problem when parents are too lenient or seldom at home to lay down and enforce rules. And children learn the lesson from parents who always feel that they are getting ripped off, that someone else is always responsible for their problems.

Family messages that encourage children to look for the easy way out go something like this:

- "No one understands us."
- "You can't succeed on your own."

- "People in our family don't fail."
- "If you do fail, don't let anyone know about it."
- "There's nothing wrong with a little white lie."
- "It's not *your* fault."
- "I want it when I want it, and I want it now!"

Jesus had something to say about people who look for the easy way out. After He told the rich young ruler to give all his wealth away and follow Him, and the rich man had gone away sorrowing, Jesus told His disciples, "How hard it is for those who have riches to enter the kingdom of God!" (Mark 10:23). Hard, yes. But, oh, how worthwhile! The rich young ruler took the easy way out by keeping his wealth, and thus he missed out on finding truth. Taking the easy way out by keeping problems secret also prevents us from discovering truth and being fulfilled in our lives.

Secrets Are Kept Because People Are Lonely

Lonely people know they are lonely, but it's not always easy for others to detect. Some, like Vivian, don't appear to be that lonely. In school, Vivian was a cheerleader, a leader in her church youth group, and she was involved in numerous clubs and school activities. Vivian lonely? Impossible! What no one knew was that her busyness was her way of compensating for the loneliness of her home life.

You see, Vivian's parents were workaholics who had little time for their only child. Even though her days were filled with friends and activities, she suffered from a lack of love from her parents. Today Vivian is addicted to food, yet she keeps up the image she learned as a girl. She is plagued by bulimia, yet no one knows. All they see is her bubbly involvement in everything and everybody.

Other lonely people go to the opposite extreme and isolate themselves. That's how it was with Shawn. When Shawn was young, his parents divorced, and he was shuffled back and forth between them. He had trouble making friends and insists today that he has never had a close friend in his life. Shawn never managed to develop the social skills needed to make his way in the world. Perhaps that's why he chose to attend a large university where he could easily stay lost in the crowd.

Today Shawn works in a large accounting firm, where he mostly stays alone in his office cubicle and works with numbers. Anyone who comes in contact with him would describe him as lonely.

Loneliness breeds secrecy because of the perceived or actual lack of opportunity to open up to others. So what are the characteristics lonely people share? There are several characteristics:

- *They suffer from low self-esteem.* Feeling bad about themselves keeps them emotionally isolated.

- *They never learned social skills.* They don't fit in. They aren't able to interact socially with other people. They tend to stay removed and aloof, communicating only on a shallow, surface level.

- *They often prefer to interact with machines rather than with people.* Radio, television, tapes, CDs, and computers are often their favorite companions.

- *They were not emotionally close to their parents.* Lonely people often had parents who spent far more time disciplining them than playing with them, and talking at them rather than communicating with them. Many times they were raised in unstable or unrooted families.

Lonely people can be as different as Vivian is from Shawn. Their secret is *I don't know how to love, so maybe I am unlovable.* Yet they all can say with the psalmist: "Turn Yourself to me, and have mercy on me, for I am desolate and afflicted" (Ps. 25:16).

Some of the family messages that foster loneliness include:

- "Don't mind him, he's just shy."
- "If you can't say anything nice, keep your mouth shut."
- "What goes on in our family is no one else's business."
- "Children should be seen and not heard."
- "Everything you say is stupid."

In the book of Luke, we read about Jesus' interaction with one of the most lonely men of his time—Zacchaeus, the despised tax collector. Jesus appreciated and understood the depth of Zacchaeus's loneliness and isolation from other Jews. And in an amazing action for that time and culture, He restored Zacchaeus by going into his home and eating with him, the greatest way a Jew of that time could show companionship and acceptance of another person. Isolation results in a lack of in-depth conversation that exposes our true thoughts and brings our secrets out of hiding.

Every one of us has a God-given need to reach out and touch other people, emotionally, spiritually, and physically, just as we have a burning need to commune with God.

In Job 19:13–14, Job cries out: "He has removed my brothers far from me, and my acquaintances are completely estranged from me. My relatives have failed, and my close friends have forgotten me." What a poignant cry of despair! Job's family was gone and his friends had deserted him. How forgotten and forsaken he had to have felt. Poor Job was well acquainted with the loneliness that comes with losing everyone and everything he loved. But instead of letting it drive him to total despair, Job allowed his loneliness to push him to search for a deeper, truer understanding of God and His providential, all-encompassing love.

Triggers That Perpetuate the Secrets

Many people in our lives fit into the categories just discussed, yet they don't seem to have any big secrets. Remember that when we talk about secrets, they don't have to be "big" secrets, which are shameful. *Secrets* can also refer to situations that are known but never discussed or acknowledged.

Both Mary Ann and Bob know that Mary Ann makes a much higher salary than Bob. It isn't a secret in the sense that no one knows. What makes it a secret, and destructive, is that they never discuss their feelings about it. Mary Ann has no idea how uncomfortable Bob feels. If they don't discuss this secret it may wreck their marriage.

Certainly not everyone who feels guilty and ashamed, is afraid of failing, escapes reality, fears intimacy, takes the easy way out, or is lonely is hiding secrets. But such people certainly are at risk for becoming secret-keepers, given the right trigger.

What might this trigger be? It can be an emotional stressor, fear, a loss, or a significant life change.

Emotional Stressors

Just what constitutes an emotional stressor is difficult to say, for it varies from person to person. It depends on a specific individual's weak point or Achilles heel. Some common stressors are:

* Job stresses
* Marriage or home problems

- Conflicts in any area of life
- Financial problems
- Inability to achieve at school, at work, or in another area of performance
- Discontent with current lifestyle or living conditions.

Consider the differences between Peggy's stressors and Matt's. Peggy was a full-time mom, a full-time wife, and a part-time employee. She never did enough to be the kind of mom, wife, and employee she wanted to be. Because she felt guilty about the time her job took away from her family, she wouldn't ask her husband and children to pitch in and help at home.

Unfortunately, Peggy was trying to be the same kind of mother her mother had been—but her mother had never worked outside the home. The perfectly kept house, the homecooked meals, the homebaked bread, and the starched and ironed clothes that Peggy remembered from her childhood haunted her and made her feel guilty for the things she just didn't have time to do for her own family. Peggy was so stressed out that she was quickly becoming addicted to the prescription drugs her doctor gave her to calm her nerves.

Things were different for Matt. He had a full-time job, a wife and five children to support, and was in graduate school. Although he was overwhelmed and exhausted from the load he was carrying, when asked to teach a Sunday school class, he couldn't say no. Matt desperately wanted to be an understanding husband, a terrific father, a straight-A student, and an ever-available lay worker at church. But it just was not possible to do it all.

Matt's father was a critical man who loved his son but who always demanded the best from him. It took a lot of work to free Matt from his generational cycle of trying to be everything to everybody.

Peggy's stressor was conflict between job and home. Matt's stressor was that he was addicted to pleasing people.

Fear

Fear can work both ways: It motivates some people to reach beyond themselves and accomplish more than they ever thought they could, but other people are paralyzed by it.

Gary and Susan were a young married couple who enjoyed playing tennis together. Back in high school, Gary had been an all-state quarterback, but after he and Susan were married he became even more obsessed with health and physical fitness. Even though Susan was a beautiful young woman with an almost perfect figure, Gary began to tease her about needing to lose a few pounds and to tighten up a few muscles. Out of her fear of being abandoned, Susan tried to go along with her husband. Although she was always on a diet and involved in some new exercise program, she felt more and more self-conscious about her appearance—especially when she was around Gary.

"I don't want to undress in front of him," she said,

"or even to wear anything that is the least bit revealing. I know he'll start criticizing me." And how was this affecting them as a couple? "We have very little sex life," Susan said sadly. "And it's mainly my fault."

That's how Gary saw it, too. And when the secret of his affair with a bean-pole-thin clerk in his law office was discovered, he justified it by pointing directly at Susan.

In therapy Gary and Susan began to understand the roots of Gary's addiction to exercise and Susan's terror of being abandoned if she failed to be exactly what her husband wanted her to be. In their case, fear was a big part of their secrecy and resulting lack of intimacy. Once they understood what was going on, Susan and Gary were finally in a position to make some changes.

Fear can take many forms. It can be a fear of failure —of not measuring up. It can be a fear of rejection, a fear of setting boundaries, or a fear of accepting a relationship that might turn out to be painful—a fear of being hurt. It can be a fear that God "doesn't love me," or that He "could never forgive me." It can be a fear of disaster, or of illness, or of death. An increasingly common fear in our society is a fear of growing old and losing the youthful looks that we believe make us valuable.

Fear can also be a trigger to motivate. David, who God described as "a man after my own heart," knew something about motivating fear. His fear against Goliath pushed him to seek God and watch God's strength destroy the enemy. Peter did a great job of walking out to Jesus on the water—until he took his eyes off Jesus and looked down at the waters around him and started to sink. His fear forced him to cry out to Jesus, and Peter was saved. It was Moses' fear that caused him to beg, "Lord, send somebody to Pharaoh other than me." But when he moved beyond focusing on his own weaknesses and learned to depend instead on God's strengths, his fear motivated his accomplishments that were to change the world. David and Moses moved ahead with their fear while Peter allowed the fear to paralyze him.

Are you allowing your fear to paralyze you, or are you using it to motivate you? If you are looking to yourself for strength, you can expect paralysis. It is in looking to God that you will find motivation.

Loss

Sam's dad, a workaholic, had drilled his philosophy of life into Sam at a tender age: "If you work hard enough and play by the rules, you will be a success in life." As an Army officer, Sam had worked hard and he had carefully played by the rules. In fact, the military had been his whole life until cutbacks had forced him into early retirement at the age of forty-five. His job gone and his sense of identity with it, Sam sank into a deep depression.

Never more than a social drinker, Sam was rapidly becoming addicted to alcohol, the secret he carefully hid from family and friends. "It isn't fair!" he cried out again and again. "Life just isn't fair!"

He's right. Life isn't fair. Unfortunately, Sam had been raised to believe that it is.

Loss can easily be a trigger for family secrets, just as it triggered Sam's alcohol addiction.

Loss may come in the form of personal tragedy—the death of someone close, divorce, or an accident. Or it can come in the form of lost dreams, in the death of a vision. It may be the loss of the dream of an "ideal" parent—the realization that you never will be loved the way you always wanted to be loved.

"I just want to be normal," says eighteen-year-old Candace. "But I'm not, and I never will be. I'll always be handicapped." What is her handicap? She is dyslexic. Yes, it is a problem, but not as much as Candace thinks it to be. She sees it as the loss of a vision.

Kara suffers the loss of a different kind of vision. "When I was very young, just eleven or twelve, I dreamed of the wonderful man I would someday marry," Kara says. "He would be handsome and rich, and he would spoil me with love. Well, it didn't happen. I married Richard. We divorced last year." A depression has swept over Kara that she can't shake. Not only has she experienced the loss of her marriage, but she has seen her dream die, too.

Significant Life Changes

Changes, whether large or small, are a part of life, and they are all stressors. The problem comes when we have undergone changes, but have never dealt with them emotionally. Sometimes these significant changes took place when we were children.

Significant changes fall into two main categories: *developmental changes* and *non-developmental changes.*

Developmental changes

Developmental changes are normal and natural. They include going through adolescence, leaving the security of home (and in some cases, the strong control of parents), marriage, parenthood, the loss of youth, and the "empty nest" syndrome. So if they are normal, what's the problem? Audra is a good example.

Audra has been praised all her life for her vivacious good looks. Now she is approaching her fortieth birthday. "Everybody gets older," she said lightly. "What's the big deal?"

But her behavior is saying something else. Audra is fast becoming addicted to shopping sprees. She is filling her closet with youthful-looking clothes, and she is spending a fortune on cosmetics. "They'll keep the compliments coming," she says with a laugh.

Certainly there is nothing wrong with wanting to look our best. Most of us have that desire. But for Audra, her self-esteem depends on what is on the outside rather than who she is on the inside.

The stage was set early for Audra. From her earliest memories, she recalls her father making comments about beautiful women. And Audra's mother always took great pains to look "just right for Daddy." At the age of twenty, Audra married a man who put great value on physical appearance. "I used to ask him if he would have courted me if I wasn't pretty, and he always said, 'Court you! I'd never have given you a second glance!' "

For Audra, the loss of her youthful attractiveness is a trigger that set off the secret of uncontrollable shopping. "I hide the bills from my husband," she admits. "So far I've managed to pay them off without him knowing, but. . . ."

Non-Developmental changes

Margaret and Ed had lived in the same town their entire married life, nearly eleven years, when Ed's company transferred him unexpectedly. They had to leave their church, all their friends, and the children's school. It wasn't so bad for Ed since he had his new job, and the children adjusted quickly. But Margaret felt lost and lonely in the strange new town. She just couldn't shake the overwhelming sadness and seething anger the move had caused her.

In an attempt to quiet her loneliness, Margaret telephoned her sister and best friend back home and talked for hours. "I just had to talk to someone who cared about my pain and loneliness," she said. But she was careful to hide both her anger and the mounting bills from her husband.

Moving, changing jobs (even positive events, such as getting a promotion), or losing a good friend or family member due to a move—can all trigger secrets.

Self-Fulfilling Prophecies

Brad's grandfather was a big fellow, weighing in at well over three hundred pounds. All his life Brad was told, "You are going to be just like your grandfather." Now at age thirty Brad is well on his way.

Brad hadn't grown up heavy. Only after he graduated from college and faced the stresses of marriage and a new job with a paycheck that just didn't reach far enough did he begin to see the fulfillment of the family prophecy.

"I put on sixty pounds in six months," Brad said. "I'd always been told that was how I would deal with stress, and sure enough, when the pressures came, Grandfather climbed right up on my back and those prophecies were fulfilled."

Our families have an uncanny way of programming negatives into us.

- "You will never amount to anything."
- "You could have done better."
- "You can't lose weight."
- "You are bad!"
- "You're just like your father (uncle, sister, grandmother)!"

When you hear something again and again and again, you begin to believe it. And when you keep on hearing it, it eventually becomes a part of who you are. And you start to say:

- "I can't help it. That's just the way I am."
- "I'm no good. The only way I'll ever get anyone to love me is to give in to him sexually."
- "Everybody takes advantage of me."
- "I am so hopelessly overscheduled, and I can't do everything I've already committed myself to. But, okay, I guess I'll try to squeeze in that one more thing."

What we fill our minds with is what we are sure to become. What we are told, what we believe, becomes a self-fulfilling prophecy.

Making It Personal

Those who are trapped cannot do anything about the secrets that are being harbored until they understand them. The following questions can help determine where those secrets are coming from.

- Am I feeling ashamed and guilty?
- Am I afraid of looking like a failure?
- Am I trying to escape from reality?
- Do I fear intimacy?
- Do I tend to look for the easy way out?
- Am I lonely?

Once the source of the secret is determined, it is crucial to see what is causing you to keep the secret. Could it be:

- emotional stressors?
- a recent loss?
- significant life changes that are taking place?
- self-fulfilling prophecies?

Whatever the reason for the secrets, one thing is certain: Secrets do not easily come to an end. Unless someone steps forward to break the power of the secret, it will continue to plague a family generation after generation after generation. But that one person can break the secret.

The way to start is to admit the secret. This is the only way to break the power of the secret.

Next, the approach must be in a way that will restore relationships—especially the relationship to God. The intent is not to hang out all the family wash for everyone to see. The search is for the truth, and the goal is to live in this truth.

Finally, the secret-breaker can trust God with the outcome. The temptation will be to get discouraged when everything doesn't all get fixed immediately. But this is only the beginning.

3

From Generation to Generation

I am so sad and lonely all the time," Jenna told us. "I don't know why. I just feel like bad things are going to happen to me and the people I love."

Jenna's husband Bill had encouraged her to come into therapy because their seven-year-old daughter Kelly was having trouble sleeping through the night. Every few hours the child was awakened with terrifying dreams.

"I'm sure it's Jenna's own fears that are causing it," Bill confided to us. "She is afraid of everything. She won't let Kelly out of her sight."

In talking to Jenna, we learned that years ago her older sister had drowned at a Sunday school picnic. Her devastated parents never talked about the incident. "It was just too sad," Jenna explained.

Not only was Jenna carrying her parents' pain, she was passing that pain on to little Kelly. Without help, Kelly would almost certainly pass the family legacy along to her own child.

Fortunately, that won't happen. Both Jenna and

Kelly are getting the help they need to enable them to face their fears.

The Law of the Harvest

One generation sows a secret, the next reaps the harvest. And as the secret keeps going, it gains in power. The law of the harvest proclaims: You reap what you sow, you reap in kind, and the harvest is greater than what was planted. Let's see how this law applied in Jenna's family.

You Reap What You Sow

Jenna's parents planted fear and sadness. They didn't mean to, but because they would not talk about their feelings of guilt, the "if only's," and their overwhelming feelings of grief, they sowed unresolved grief and sadness. Jenna reaped the harvest, and in turn sowed seeds of fear and anxiety that little Kelly was beginning to reap.

You Reap in Kind

If you plant an acorn, you don't grow a mesquite tree. Only oak trees grow from acorns. According to the law of the harvest, you reap in kind, and this is just as true of emotions as it is of trees.

Everyone in their small town knew that Jenna's sister had drowned, yet it was a secret because her parents wouldn't talk about it. The heartbroken parents continued to sow grief and fear, and the harvest of grief and fear continued through Jenna and Kelly.

The Harvest Is Greater than What Was Planted

"My parents loved me dearly. They would never have hurt me or Kelly in any way," said Jenna. "I'm sure they were stoic and silent about their grief because that was the way they thought good Christians were supposed to be."

Jenna's parents had been overprotective and strict throughout her teen years. "I was sure it was because they didn't trust me and thought I didn't have enough sense to make good decisions," she said. "Now I see that they were afraid of losing me, too."

What was hard to get Jenna to see was that her strict overprotectiveness was already smothering Kelly. She was doing the same thing her parents had done, only more so.

What Do Generational Secrets Look Like?

Just months after his honeymoon, Drew went on a business trip to Canada and decided to stop in and renew the acquaintance of his old girlfriend, Alicia. The two of them spent the next several days—and nights—together. Nine months later Alicia gave birth to a baby girl. The next year, Drew and his wife got a divorce.

Every month Drew took money out of his checking account and sent it to Alicia for the support of their child, yet no one in his family ever mentioned the baby.

That's the way Drew wanted it. At the very beginning he had said to his mother, "So far as the family is concerned, there is no child. Don't ever bring the subject up again."

Now, suddenly things seem to have changed. Drew recently saw his daughter, who is now ready for first grade, and has fallen in love with her. "She called me *Daddy*," he told his sister Tamara. "She is so cute and so sweet. I just can't keep her a secret anymore. She is too precious."

Is Drew breaking free of the secret? Not at all. The only ones he wants to know about the girl are his mother and sister. "I want to show you pictures of her," he told them, "and I want you to send gifts to her. I would do it myself, but I don't know what to get a little girl. But don't tell anyone else about her, especially not Dad."

Drew wants his mother and sister to join him in the family secret. Sound strange? To most people, maybe; but not to Drew. He was just following the precedent his father had set for him.

Drew's father had some secrets of his own. He had been married before and had several children from that marriage. Drew's mother knew about the previous marriage, but she knew nothing about the children until one fall evening. A young woman she had never seen before knocked at the door and announced, "I have come to meet my father."

It took a while before Drew and Tamara figured out what was going on. They didn't even know their father had had another wife, let alone any other children. During the next few years, they learned still more about old Dad: He had also been involved in several affairs.

Neither Drew nor Tamara ever really knew what their father did for a living. "He is in business" was all they were ever told. He always seemed to have plenty of money, and he was generous with it when he was home. Periodically, however, he would pack his suitcases and say elaborate good-byes, but he never left any money for the family. Everyone scrimped and saved, mowed lawns, and did odd jobs to keep food on the table until Dad came back home with the checkbook. Sometimes it was a few days; sometimes it was a month or so.

So to Drew, his actions did not seem all that strange. He was merely following the pattern he had learned at home.

Without a doubt, there were generational secrets in Drew's family. It's not hard to identify such secrets if you know the characteristics.

- There is dysfunction within the family.
- The family is estranged and isolated.
- Family members play roles to hide their true selves.
- The family pours its energy into keeping the secret.
- The secret-keeper holds the power within the family system.
- The family usually has more secrets lurking in the closet.

Let's look more closely at each of these characteristics.

There Is Dysfunction Within the Family

It is obvious that Drew's family was not functioning properly. Secret-keeping families seldom do. The more secrets they harbor and the longer the secrets are kept, the greater the family's need to develop and hone the defense mechanisms that allow them to cope.

It's impossible to predict what form these defense mechanisms will take, for each member of the family will come up with his or her own. Drew's defense mechanism was his rebellion. Even today he bristles at the slightest hint of authority. Tamara was a people pleaser who would do or say anything she thought others wanted her to. (She immediately went out and bought gifts for Drew's daughter and then wrapped and sent them with his name signed to the card.)

The Family Is Estranged and Isolated

The last thing secret-keeping families want is for their secrets to be discovered. The easiest way to hide what they don't want known is to keep their distance from other people, both physically and emotionally.

"When I was young, none of my friends thought it was much fun to come over to my house," Jenna said. "My mother was always watching and rushing over to do things for us. I thought she was afraid we were going to make a mess. Maybe she was just afraid something would happen to us like when my sister drowned.

Anyway, it was not much fun to play at my house." Even though everyone knew about the drowning, the family kept their pain secret.

Sometimes it is the kids who encourage the isolation. A young woman named Mary never brought friends to her home because she could never be sure how her alcoholic dad would act. Now engaged to be married, she laments, "My fiancé is getting more and more insistent about meeting my family. I've told him all about my mom and my sisters and a lot about my dad, all except his drinking. I suppose he has to be told, but I just don't know how to bring it up."

Sometimes the isolation is so subtle that other people never suspect anything is wrong. "My mother always emphasized that brothers and sisters were better off playing together than with other kids," Tamara said. "She always had some reason to discourage Drew and me from having friends over because she didn't want anyone to know Dad was an alcoholic. Drew and I knew she was protecting his temper and drinking even though we never discussed it." But even if other people don't suspect, the family members know, and they feel the estrangement.

Family Members Play Roles to Hide Their True Selves

The roles differ and the masks can be unique, but the result is always the same: Family members cannot be themselves. If Dad is a "rageaholic," for instance, his role is to stomp around yelling and raging. He is trying to cover the hidden pain of having been isolated in his family; no one knows his secret. Mother likely has to wear the mask of peacemaker. "Don't say anything to your dad," she'll caution the children, "because it will upset him." Who is the person behind Mother's mask? Who knows? She never gets to express who she really is.

The secret-keeper sets the stage, and everyone else falls in line and assumes a specific role. Drew's father left the family whenever he wanted to and gave no one an explanation for his absence. He was the undisputed boss. When his hidden family knocked on the door and his extramarital affairs came to light, no one challenged him. Mom, always the martyr, made sure everyone knew how much she was suffering. Drew rebelliously caused trouble. Tamara worked to smooth things over and make peace.

The Family Pours Its Energy into Keeping the Secret

The amount of energy families invest in secret-keeping is downright astounding. It's as if they are frantically trying to stamp out fires that are forever blazing up around them.

Remember Laura Thompson, the young woman in Chapter 1? When her family came for counseling, she had been married six months, and her marriage was already in trouble. All her emotional energy was going into playing her role and keeping the family secret. She had nothing left for her marriage. Developing a healthy relationship with a new spouse takes work, and Laura just didn't have enough energy left. Unless she freed up some energy and put it to work on her relationship with her husband, her marriage was not going to last. When Laura began to talk about the secret with her new spouse, its power was broken. Only then could Laura also talk to her family, begin to put the past behind her, and begin working on her marriage.

With the power of the family secret broken, Laura was able to do just that. But Drew, the other example, was not yet ready to rechannel the energy he was pouring into his secret.

The Secret-Keeper Holds the Power Within the Family System

In Drew and Tamara's family, their father held the power. The secrets were his, and he kept them carefully hidden away. People who hold the secrets control the situation.

In many cases, this is exactly why a person *does* hold a secret. He or she *likes* having that power. A rageaholic father is a good example. He fears that someone will find out his deep insecurities. So while he rages at home, when he is out in public, he behaves perfectly. He may not be able to control anything else in the world, but he sure can control his family. If wife or son or daughter dare to confront him, he blows up and rages on and on until he gets that person back into control. And woe be to anyone who dares to talk outside the family about Dad's temper. For if the secret were broken, he would have *no* control over *anything*.

He knows that he is out of control on the inside; that exposure would only prove his worthlessness.

The Family Usually Has More Secrets Lurking in the Closet

Secrets beget secrets. When a family holds to a secret, other secrets follow naturally. It is no surprise to learn that Drew's father already had other secrets: other children and extramarital affairs. The more secrets there are involved, the more complicated the family dynamics become.

Generational patterns of secrets look something like figure 3.1.

Secrets Are Generational

Without a doubt, secrets that are not revealed and dealt with tend to be repeated in the next generation. Secrets are unfinished business, and unfinished business carries on from one generation to another.

As discussed in Chapter 1, if you are reared with secrets, you grow up with the same insecurities and fears your family members before you had. They didn't know how to deal with them, so they were not able to teach you. People raised with the secret of incest pass it along because they have never learned how to deal in a healthy way with someone of the opposite sex. People raised with abuse secrets pass the abuse along because they never learned the give and take that is required in healthy relationships. People raised with addiction

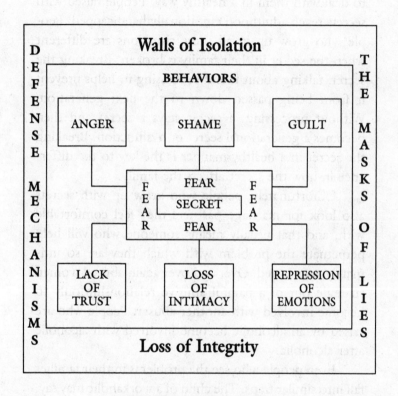

Figure 3.1

secrets, financial secrets, or secrets of grief and loss pass those problems along because they have never learned to deal with them in a healthy way. People raised with secrets reach adulthood emotionally handicapped. People who grow up in all these situations are different when the secret in their family is broken. Breaking the secret, talking about it and processing it, helps prevent it from being passed down to the next generation. Without processing, a secret stays a secret and then becomes a generational secret or dysfunction. Breaking the secret in a healthy manner is the key to the difference in how the secret affects the family.

Unfortunately, people who grow up with secrets also look for marriage partners they feel comfortable with, and that usually means someone who will help perpetuate the problem with which they are so intimately acquainted. Over and over again abused women struggle out of a painful abusive relationship only to become involved with another abuser. People who are raised by an alcoholic become involved with alcoholic after alcoholic.

Even people who see the problems in their families fall into similar traps. The child of a workaholic may say, "I'll never spend all my time at the office. My first priority will be to spend time with my children." So what happens? That person doesn't become a workaholic. He comes home from the office right at five o'clock every evening. But he doesn't spend time with his kids, either. Instead, he hides out in his workshop, or he plays golf, or he watches television. He isn't a workaholic, yet he ends up in the same place as his father—distanced from his children. And he never can understand how he got there.

What makes it so natural for a secret to move along generationally is the fact that whatever children are raised with seems normal to them. One woman said, "I'm so used to being depressed, I don't even know what it's like to feel any other way."

She was given a homework assignment: Do something fun with your husband.

The woman looked blankly. "Do something fun?" she asked. She was so used to being unhappy and depressed that the very suggestion stopped her in her tracks.

The Generational Cost of Keeping the Secret

When Ellie came for counseling, she was suffering symptoms of depression: She couldn't concentrate, she was overwhelmed by feelings of sadness, and she was eating too much. The first thing this attractive young woman did was apologize for being overweight. Obviously this caused her a great deal of embarrassment. Then, with tears streaming down her face, she told us how worthless she felt. "I'm miserable the way I am!" she sobbed.

As her story emerged, it became clear that she was paying the belated costs of her family's secret.

The Family Loses Its Realness

Because of the lies and resulting cover-ups, individuals in secret-keeping families lose their integrity—not only personal integrity, but also integrity in the sense of being real and whole, of knowing who they are. So much of what others see in secret-keepers is not who they are but who they want other people to think they are. Only when a person tells the secret can she get that integrity back.

Trust Is Lost

Ellie's paternal grandfather had embezzled a large sum of money from his employer and had been arrested at home. His son (Ellie's father, Frank), who was only eight years old at the time, had looked on in confused horror as his father was taken to jail. In anger and humiliation, young Frank had vowed that he would have nothing more to do with his father, and furthermore, that no one in his family would ever disgrace him again. When Frank grew up, he became a policeman whose job it was to enforce the law. It was his way of "undoing" the sins of his father. Frank did not talk about his father or share his pain with the family. He mistrusted people and suspected them of being dishonest.

"My father never did trust me," Ellie said sadly. Ellie's father didn't even trust his daughter, which gave her feelings of self-doubt and insecurity.

Such families don't know whom they can trust

anymore, and this uncertainty only serves to empower and strengthen the secret. In time the perception becomes a self-fulfilling prophecy, and soon there is a complete lack of trust.

Here's an example of how this works. Stephanie had gotten into trouble for writing bad checks. "I tried to tell her that women cannot be trusted with finances," her husband said.

That's what he believed, and he convinced Stephanie that it was true. In time, it became reality. When the bad check problem surfaced, he told her, "Fine. I'll keep the checkbook and you'll never have access to it again." Stephanie's secret is that her family placed women in a second-class role and treated them as if they couldn't handle financial matters. So Stephanie assumed this role. Her husband's family had the same type of beliefs about women and money. Stephanie and her husband challenged this secret in therapy.

In therapy, Stephanie's husband agreed that he loved his wife too much to let money come between them. To prove it, he gave her back her checkbook. Sure enough, she wrote a few more bad checks. This time, however, her husband told her that she would have to go to the bank and take care of the problem herself. She did. It took months, but eventually Stephanie's husband regained respect for his wife, and she gained new respect for herself. Because they were willing to work at redirecting their thinking, Stephanie and her husband were able to build up a whole new level of trust between them. After four years, Stephanie assumed the job of keeping the books for her husband's multimillion dollar business.

Family Members' Feelings Are Denied and Repressed

The more Ellie talked, the more she recalled the old pain she had repressed for so long. "My father is a good man!" she insisted over and over. Encouraged to talk more about him, she added, "The problem was, he was always angry. And he worked all the time. I don't really remember him being home very much."

Asked to tell of a time when she and her father were together, she recounted the following.

"Once when I was thirteen, I had my friend Annette over to my house to spend the night. Her brother came over to bring us a pizza, and the three of us sat around in my room eating pizza and talking. My dad came home early from his night shift and found us in my room. He threw my friend's brother out; then he grabbed me and slapped me across the face and told me I was acting like a slut. I felt so bad and so frightened and so guilty."

She had forgotten that vivid incident for years. The secret of Frank's father was especially hurtful because Ellie never understood why her own father did not trust her. She simply accepted the self-fulfilling prophecy: *I can't be trusted. I must be bad.*

The Pattern Is Carried On

Ellie was a perfect example of a self-fulfilling prophecy that had its roots two generations before. "Two years after the incident with my friend's brother, my best friend Gloria's older brother raped me," Ellie said. "Terrified and hysterical, I figured that just proved my dad was right. I really was a slut. So I went on having sex with the boy, mainly because I didn't know how to stop it."

At the age of sixteen, Ellie ran away and married a wild young man who turned out to be a drug dealer. He was abusive toward her, frequently beating her up. It took her two years to get up the courage to leave him and go back home.

Ellie grew up not being trusted, undergoing constant questioning, and being accused of all sorts of immoral thoughts and behavior. And for years, she lived out those accusations. Frank couldn't trust his father, so he vowed not to get hurt. He raised Ellie by criticizing her all the time. She then had self-doubt and acted out the negative feelings passed on to her.

Not all examples are so dramatic. "When we were married, my husband insisted that all our money was mine as much as it was his," said Nora. "But right away he insisted that we buy a house to live in and a second one as an investment. I was terrified. Here I was just twenty-two, and we had spent all our money on two houses I hadn't even wanted in the first place!"

But there was a lot more going on than just the

houses. Nora's husband's generational pattern was to handle situations with raging anger while keeping them secret within the family. No one outside the family ever heard the ugly words of Nora's father-in-law or those of her husband. Nora's family kept her father's extramarital affairs secret. Nora didn't trust men, and with that mistrust she was easily able to trigger her husband's rage.

"I could see that something very unpleasant was happening in our marriage," said Nora, "but I didn't know what to do about it. I figured, I'm unhappy just like my parents were unhappy. This marriage is not working out, and I don't like it."

What Nora was doing was following right along in line with her mother's training: *Get a career, and don't put up with any man making you unhappy.*

"Actually, my mother thought she was breaking the family pattern," she added. "She was speaking to me about it, and giving me what she thought was good advice."

Openness and Intimacy Are Lost

Ellie's father Frank was a good, honest, churchgoing man who truly cared about his daughter. Unfortunately, he was not able to convey his loving concern to her. His own secret held him captive to the belief that to open up and care about people would surely lead to betrayal.

Nora's mother cared a great deal about her, too.

More than anything, she wanted her daughter to lead a happier life than she herself had led.

"When I got married, it was like a business deal," Nora says. "I had a checklist to help me evaluate exactly what I wanted out of the relationship. I asked my husband, 'Okay, what did your dad do to you when you were little?' I wanted to know what excess baggage he might be bringing into a marriage. Then I said, 'Take me to your home, I want to meet your parents.' He did, and I was impressed by how nice they were to me. So I figured, Okay, this guy doesn't drink and he goes to church, so he isn't likely to end up hurting me. I think he will do. He'll be a good one to break this generational thing from my own family."

While the approach may have made good business sense, it surely kept all openness and intimacy out of the marriage. This allowed those old secrets to march right in and take over.

As for Ellie, as she began to understand the power her father's secret had had in her family, and how it was affecting her, she made the decision to take control. She was finally able to break away from her fulfillment of that old prophecy, but it required several years and a great deal of painful work. She also talked with her father, and together they are working toward forgiveness and healing. When learned patterns of behavior are destructive and are never recognized for the harm they do, they become secrets that are passed down generationally. When the secret and shame are revealed, family

members begin to understand each other and the healing can begin.

Words of Direction

The apostle Paul wrote: "Let no one deceive you
with empty words, for because of these things the wrath
of God comes. . . . Therefore do not be partakers
with them. For you were once darkness, but now you
are light in the Lord. Walk as children of light. And
have no fellowship with the unfruitful works of darkness, but rather expose them" (Eph. 5:6–8, 11).

Chapter 2 spoke of beginning as a secret-breaker.
As a child of light, here are encouraging points to keep
in mind.

- At any point in the generations of a secret, a pattern
  of dysfunction can be broken and changed. It is as
  simple as refusing to pass the secret along.
- Once the secret has been exposed to the light of
  truth, by dealing with the pain and practicing
  healthy behaviors, healing will cover all that past
  darkness.
- Secrets aren't all that are generational. Practicing
  truth and healing are generational as well. Being
  honest and up-front with children will encourage
  them to grow up practicing honesty and openness
  to the generation that follows them.
- There is no best timing or perfect situation—except
  now. Confronting secrets encourages changing

those personality characteristics that perpetuate the secrets.

- Resting in the knowledge that the healing and renewal Jesus Christ provides will give the strength to break generational patterns and live secret-free.

4

Addiction Secrets

Sharon's father was an alcoholic who neglected his wife and children. He was never around for any of his daughter's activities. "He always promised me he would be at my dance recitals and school programs," Sharon said, "but he never came. Again and again and again he broke his promises to me. I guess it all seemed trivial to him, but to me it meant everything."

Even though Sharon learned not to trust men, she ended up marrying Eric, a very dependable man who was the complete opposite of her father. The only problem was that Eric was a workaholic. He neglected his family, too. To Sharon, it felt like life with her father all over again.

Sharon and Eric have a daughter, Diane, who feels just as hurt about all her father's broken promises as Sharon felt years before. Now fourteen, Diane has developed an addiction of her own—not to alcohol or to work, but to food. She has watched her dad model coping by escape, and she is doing the same thing.

All addictions have the same root secret: denial.

This is the insistence that "I'm not really doing what I'm doing." Addictions have something else in common: they are all based on unresolved emotions— shame, hurt, anger, and fear of being hurt still more.

The great irony of addiction is that the very thing the addicted person is after is what that person is going to lose. Diane wants a relationship with her father. But by overeating she is making herself "less lovable" by her appearance and isolating herself even more.

The Cost of Addictions

Addictions do not come cheap. The high cost includes:

- *A loss of relationships.* This can be more than just a loss of relationships with other people. It can include the loss of a relationship with God.

- *Problems with intimacy.* This may take the form of not being able to be intimate with other people, or it may be a craving for inappropriate intimacy.

- *Financial disaster.* Many people with addictions totally lose any financial security. This can include job loss, the loss of an inheritance, or the loss of a career.

- *Physical problems.* These can come in the form of physical illness (such as ulcers or heart problems), in the form of sexual problems, or as in the loss of appearance (eating disorders is a good example).

- *Psychological problems.* These can include depression, low self-esteem, anxiety, and an impaired ability to make decisions.

- *Spiritual problems.* Addicted people who do not know God are cut off from Him. Those who do know God *feel* as though they are cut off from Him.

Often, addicted people are the last ones to see the high price they are paying. Reed-thin anorexics insist they are still too heavy; bulimics cannot see the ravages of their condition that cause them to look years older than their age; alcoholics argue that it's "not liquor, just beer and wine." Addicted people are often the last to admit there is a problem and to realize others have discovered the secret.

Very often, the final cost of addiction is shattered lives.

Types of Addictions

People can become involved in a wide variety of addictions, and it is quite common for people to have multiple addictions. A man who is addicted to drugs may also be a rageaholic. A woman may be addicted to food and to shopping.

Most people see alcoholism, drug abuse, sexual addiction, and gambling as problems that need to be dealt with. But other addictions are difficult to confront because they are so subtle. Some are activities that in moderation are actually good, even necessary. A workaholic, for instance, insists, "I'm just meeting my family's financial needs. I'm just being a good provider." People carry on addictive behaviors because they are unwilling to look at the secrets behind the addiction. The addicted person may not want to change anything, and those around the person may just want to treat the addiction and not the secrets.

"Churchaholism" is an especially tough addiction to confront. Is it really possible to serve God too much? Certainly the first and greatest commandment is to love God with all our hearts, with all our souls, and with all our minds. But God also tells us we have a responsibility to meet the needs of our families. If a person is at church six nights a week, is that person serving God appropriately? While impressing others with their church leadership, churchaholics hide the secret that they are ignoring their families.

Here, then, are some of the most common types of addictions.

Workaholism

Workaholism is probably the most common of acceptable addictions. Workaholics attempt to escape reality by working. Their greatest satisfaction comes from achievements at work, while relationships run a distant second. Because their satisfaction comes from achievement, they simply cannot say no to another job, and overcommitment is always lurking just around the corner. Workaholics have a driving need to please others and to accomplish things, regardless of the toll it takes on their families. They keep the secret of ignoring their personal needs and their families in an effort to succeed.

(Workaholism can also show itself through overinvolvement in hobbies: watching too much television, weekends spent watching—or playing—sports, hours glued to the computer screen.)

The following questionnaire can help assess true workaholism.

WORKAHOLIC SCALE

Yes *No*

____ ____ 1. Most weeks, do you work more than 45–50 hours?

____ ____ 2. Do you tend to overcommit on projects?

____ ____ 3. Do you feel guilty when you "play"?

____ ____ 4. Does anyone in your family complain about your long hours at work?

____ ____ 5. Are you unable to spend time most nights with your spouse and children?

____ ____ 6. If you are honest with yourself, do you have to admit you don't really know your children? Are you unsure of such things as their favorite foods, who their friends are, and the classes they like best in school?

The more questions answered with a "yes," the more likely the person is a bona fide workaholic.

Workaholism affects the entire family and sets up

patterns for the generations to come. Consider these facts.

- Children follow the model of their workaholic parent, and many times they, too, become work-addicted. This becomes a family secret as one parent ignores personal needs and family without ever discussing the harm or trying to stop the cycle.
- The workaholic's spouse has emotional needs. Since the workaholic is never around, the spouse often gets those emotional needs met in unhealthy ways —through the children, other addictions, or unhealthy relationships with others. The children watch and tend to follow in their parents' footsteps.
- Children of workaholics grow up with low self-esteem, feeling that they are never able to please their parents. This feeling of "not being good enough" can carry over into the children's relationship with their heavenly Father.
- Some children of workaholics do the opposite of what they see modeled by their parents. When they grow up, they become pleasure seekers who turn away from responsibility, and even from God.

Anne is a good example of how this happens. A career woman who spends most of her time at work, Anne isn't getting her needs for intimacy met. The secret is kept in the form of denial: those around Anne know about her work habits, but she insists she's not hiding anything or doing anything wrong. Her secret is her need for intimacy. Not that a lack of intimacy is new to her. Her parents' marriage was cold and distant, with her mother and father each going their own ways and following their own interests.

Since healthy intimacy was never modeled for her, the only way Anne knows to feel good about herself is by achieving at work. And so she works—day and night, weekdays and weekends and holidays. She has never taken a vacation.

"I do a good job, and everyone at work appreciates the effort I put out," Anne insists. It's true. Everyone at the office is impressed with her hard work, and they do compliment her constantly. But since her work has become a substitute for companionship with her family and friends, and even for time she would otherwise spend on her relationship with God, Anne is a bona fide workaholic.

Drugs and Alcohol

Darlene had always been a healthy, active little girl. But when she entered adolescence, she was stricken with a case of acne that became increasingly severe. The more her face broke out, the more self-conscious and withdrawn she became. In her loneliness, Darlene turned first to alcohol and then to drugs.

Now in her thirties, Darlene is still trapped by her addictive behaviors. The problem is, she cannot forget the hurts of the past. She just can't shake her sense of worthlessness. This is complicated by the fact that she is also very angry with her parents about their attitude during that difficult time of her life. "They never tried to understand my pain," she says bitterly. "When I tried to tell them how much I longed to be pretty, they called me shallow. They were always onto me about my drinking and using drugs but they never seemed to give a second thought to how I felt." Darlene's parents wanted to discuss the drinking and drugs. But what about the secrets behind Darlene's addiction? What about the insecurity and loneliness that are tougher to talk about than the chemicals themselves? Darlene's parents didn't want to hear about any of those feelings; they preferred that she keep them secret.

The fact of the matter is that Darlene's parents probably did care, and they probably did the best they could for her. It was just that they didn't know how to help their daughter through that difficult time. Perhaps, like so many parents, they didn't feel good about themselves. If that was so, how could they help Darlene feel good about herself?

Darlene's story is not unusual for people who are addicted to drugs and alcohol. They rely on chemicals to help them deal with the feelings they can't handle alone, and they use alcohol and drugs in an attempt to numb their pain.

Rage

Most people are more familiar with the terms *alcoholic* and *workaholic* than with *rageaholic*. Yet most of us have encountered such individuals. Rageaholics are not hard to describe.

- They suffer from low self-esteem.
- They need to control others and they do so by yelling and shouting.
- They are critical.
- They strike fear into the hearts of their children.
- They are unable to deal with anger and pain.
- They are afraid of conflict.
- They never accept responsibility. ("It's not me; it's the traffic/kids/boss/stupid car/dumb dog.")

Rageaholics feel only one negative emotion: rage. Fear? It becomes rage. Pain? It becomes rage. Insecurity? It, too, becomes rage. Rageaholism is usually kept within the home; sometimes it is carried into the office, but usually not if the person can be fired. This behavior is often kept secret from friends and relatives. For example, the rageaholic might treat his or her spouse well at an outing and then get into the car and explode.

Part of the problem is that rageaholics are not able to verbalize their pain. The pain usually started in their childhood and over time has become an integral part of them. The rage acts as a catharsis for that deep-seated pain, but any relief they get lasts only a brief time. Then comes the guilt. They end up worse off than ever, because the root causes of the pain and anger have not been confronted and resolved.

Generationally, deep anger is especially hurtful be-

cause its root—the secret that caused it—keeps on man-
ifesting itself in generation after generation. It starts
with deep, unresolved pain—a parent whose death left
the family in desperate straights, for instance, or an unexpected financial calamity. When that very real loss is
not grieved and the pain is never experienced appropriately, it can easily result in an adult child whose bitterness has turned to rage. These adult children rage at
their own children, who grow up to rage in turn at *their*
children, who grow up to rage at *their* children.

"I never knew my great-grandfather, but I hear
that he was the original rageaholic," Peter says. "He
had worked hard for what he had, only to lose it all in
the Great Depression. I barely remember my grandfather, but I do recall being terrified of him. I loved my
father, but it was also true that I feared him. And it
pains me to admit that I see that same fear in the faces
of my own children."

One thing that makes rageaholics especially difficult to deal with is that *their angry tactics work*. They
really are able to control the people around them. They
do get what they want. And so the raging continues and
even escalates.

Peter grew up with an angry, cursing father. He
blamed, he screamed and yelled, and he was quick to
condemn. Today Peter is so afraid of being blamed if
something doesn't go exactly right that he quickly
jumps in and loudly blames someone else first. It is his
way of protecting himself.

"My father raged at me and slapped me around,"

Peter says. "As a little kid I felt crummy and worthless. As I grew older, all I felt was anger at the world." In Peter's family, the original secret is *We lost our money, so now we are worthless.* That feeling of worthlessness and the rage it brings is being handed down to each generation.

When Peter began taking his anger out on his children, his wife confronted him with what he was doing. "I loved my father," Peter says. "But I also feared him, and at times I even hated him. When my wife confronted me, I just couldn't stand the thought of my kids feeling toward me the way I felt toward my father."

Today Peter is working at dealing with his anger and moving toward forgiveness. He is determined that the problem will be settled before he condemns his own children to carry on the angry family legacy.

Many rageaholic men defend themselves by insisting that they are merely acting like "real men," that only wimps go placidly through life without a fight. God doesn't agree. In the Scriptures we read:

> "For the wrath of man does not produce the righteousness of God" (James 1:20).

> "Let all bitterness, wrath, anger, clamor, and evil speaking be put away from you, with all malice" (Eph. 4:31).

Real *healthy* men (and women) do not control others with their rage.

Compulsive Shopping

Eighteen-year-old Gail was raised by a workaholic mother who paid little attention to her daughter—except for her appearance. "My mom was always busy," Gail says. "About the only time we spent together was when she would take me shopping for clothes. But I always knew Mom loved me because she spent so much money on me."

While Gail has learned little about achieving intimacy through sharing thoughts, concerns, joys, and problems, she has learned to value bulging dresser drawers and a closet stuffed with clothes. Much of the spending was hidden, but even more, the lack of intimacy was kept secret and never acknowledged.

Gail came from a long line of people who didn't know how to express love in an appropriate way. Her grandmother worked on the farm beside her husband, and she gardened and raised chickens. She took great pride in her state fair prize-winning jams and jellies. With all this, she had little time left for her daughter who, she firmly believed, should be seen and not heard.

Because Gail's mother had felt so neglected as a child, she tried to do better with her daughter. But as Gail became an out-of-control shopaholic, her mother grew worried. "Gail is driving me so deeply into debt buying all those clothes and shoes and everything that I'll never be able to pay the bills!" her mother said in exasperation.

"But I have to look nice," Gail protested. "And I

want to get nice presents for my friends and family. I want them to know I care about them."

With shopaholics, there is always some reason to buy. There was a sale on furniture. Books improve the mind. The children needed new toys. But whatever the excuse, the real reason for buying is to prove self-worth: *If I have plenty of things, then I must be worthwhile.*

Ironically, shopaholics can come from penny-pinching families, too. They firmly believe that the world owes them. Ron fits right into this category.

When Ron was a boy, his father was well known for being a miser. "I'm not paying for new clothes for that boy until he can no longer get into the ones he has!" Ron's father would exclaim. So poor little Ronnie went to school with patched jeans several inches above his ankles, thread-bare shirts, mismatched socks, and too-small shoes with holes in the toes.

Today, Ron's seething anger is apparent at the mention of his father. "I was humiliated by that cheap old man!" he says. How is Ron handling that anger? He spends far too much money on his clothes, on his hobbies, on everything. Spending is his attempt to feel better about himself. And, as he likes to insist, "Why not buy what I want? I deserve it!" Most addictions stem from the secret feeling *I am worthless.*

People addicted to shopping or to spending money have a constant need for approval and attention. Again, this pattern, usually set in childhood, is carried down through the generations as parents model to their children that money can be a substitute for love, time, and caring. The secret continues on until someone faces the truth that money is a poor replacement for love, approval, and attention, and that it never will be able to fill the emptiness within.

Shopaholism can also be brought on by a particular life change. More and more these days, normal developmental changes are handled with addictive behaviors. That stage of life known as mid-life crisis is a good example.

Instead of mid-life crises being limited to men nearing forty, it is common for men all the way from thirty to sixty to struggle with the changes in their lives. Some resort to such behaviors as overspending, becoming involved in sexual affairs, getting divorces after years of marriage, or distancing themselves emotionally—sometimes even physically—from their wives and children.

Changes such as marriage (or remarriage) and parenthood can trigger overspending, too. Wayne is a good example.

Wayne was both elated and frightened by the birth of his first child. Although he hated to admit it, at times the idea of marriage and becoming a parent left him feeling trapped. He was only thirty-three years old, yet he could already see that he wasn't going to be the great business success he had always dreamed of being. So what did Wayne do? He bought a shiny red sports car, had his hair styled in an expensive salon, and bought himself a new wardrobe of "with it" clothes.

His wife, Elaine, pleaded for answers. "Why is my

husband suddenly spending so much money? We can't afford it and he knows it! I just can't understand what is happening. Wayne seems to be changing before my very eyes!"

What was happening was that the significant changes in Wayne's life were overwhelming him, and this was triggering his overspending. Instead of confronting those changes, he was quickly becoming addicted to the high that comes with extravagant spending.

"Wayne is getting to be just like his dad," Elaine said sadly. "Whenever my father-in-law gets stressed, he buys himself new toys. When Wayne, his youngest, left home, his dad bought himself a boat. When Wayne's father was forced into retirement, he bought a motorcycle. Wayne's mother tells me it has caused trouble between the two of them their entire married life."

Eating Disorders

Eating disorders are becoming more and more common in this country. They come in many forms and affect a staggering number of people. People are secretive about their eating disorders, but soon others start to notice the ravages of anorexia. Since the effects of bulimia are not as noticeable, often bulimics can keep their secret a long while. Compulsive overeaters may have a visible weight gain but still not reveal their secret compulsion to overeat nearly every day of their lives.

Fifteen-year-old Luanne, a tiny wisp of a girl, suffers from an eating disorder. She has been anorexic since she was twelve. Nineteen-year-old Kate, a tan, normal-sized college sophomore, also has an eating disorder. She is bulimic.

Eating disorders seem to run in the Anderson family, and it is the men who are the most affected. The way Anderson men deal with stress is to overeat. From Grandpa, to Dad and his brothers, to teenagers Don and Gene, they range from seventy-five to one hundred fifty pounds overweight. Little Philip, only eight, has been grossly overweight all his life. "Eat up!" he was always told. "Eat like a man!" And that's what he did—he ate like an Anderson man.

In the eyes of the Anderson family, "a healthy appetite" is the mark of a real man. All family activities, celebrations, and holidays are centered around huge meals, with pies and cakes for dessert and an endless supply of snacks.

"There are a few fat people in our family," Grandpa Anderson concedes, "but they are all women."

Overeating

This is certainly the most common of the eating disorders. Experts tell us that approximately 34 million American adults are overweight—51 percent of the population. Although obesity in our society is represented in every race and nationality, every age group, every socioeconomic class, and in both sexes, there are some characteristics overeaters share. Most tend to:

- have poor eating habits
- turn to food instead of facing their feelings
- be comforted by eating
- be following in the footsteps of their parents
- eat to cover up their hurts and pain
- fear relationships with the opposite sex
- be angry

Anorexia

Anorexics are so consumed with the need to "lose weight" that they literally starve themselves, sometimes to death. In our society, it is much more acceptable for men to be overweight than women, which may be why most anorexics are young women. But older women and even men and boys can suffer from this extremely serious eating disorder.

Anorexics may share some or all of the following characteristics. Sometimes they:

- put an emphasis on appearance in general and on slimness in particular
- tend to be perfectionists
- have a need to be in control ("Other people may control me in every other way, but at least I control what I put into my body.")
- desire to shrink away
- fear becoming, or being, grown women
- have a parent who is a chronic dieter
- harbor such emotions as anger or fear

- may have suffered abuse, either emotional, physical or sexual
- fear failure

Judy Falcone's parents—an accountant father and an interior designer mother—were successful in their careers. They both were also domineering people. There was a lot of stress in the Falcone family, and a lot of pressure on Judy to be popular, to make good grades, and to be attractive (which meant staying thin). Poor Judy didn't know how to cope with it all.

When Judy was a pudgy seventh-grader, her parents gave her a birthday present of two weeks at an exclusive—and extremely expensive—"fat farm." When she got home, her parents were pleased at her new svelte figure. "You look so wonderful!" her mother said enthusiastically. "I always knew there was a beautiful girl under all that fat, and now we can finally see her."

Judy loved the attention and compliments that came her way, so she kept on with the regimen of dieting and exercising. And she kept on losing weight. She ate less and less, and exercised more and more, and she lost still more weight. Now fifteen, Judy is five foot four and weighs eighty-five pounds. Her parents are concerned.

"What's your problem?" Judy replies. "Look at the models in all the magazines. They are a lot thinner than I am. I need to lose a little more weight to look really good."

Bulimia

In some ways Cammie's story is similar to Judy's. Her father, too, is a workaholic, a successful business-man and owner of two large companies.

Cammie approached junior high school almost a hundred pounds heavier than her fashion-minded mother thought was acceptable. Cammie, like Judy, was sent to a "summer camp for young girls with problems like hers."

Cammie lost close to seventy pounds that summer, so two years later, before she entered high school, her parents sent her again. She came home that September a slim, tanned, stunning beauty.

But there was an unexpected problem. Cammie, always having been overweight, had never been accepted by the other kids at school. She had never learned any socialization skills. Now here she was, a beautiful new student at an exclusive high school, who was totally clueless about how to deal appropriately with other people. As the pressure set in, Cammie went back to her old habits of bingeing. But because she felt her thinness was all she had going for her, she also began a regimen of purging.

Cammie's date calendar was always full; she was popular with both boys and girls, but she just couldn't handle it. The boys quickly pegged her as "an easy mark" who would say yes to anything. The girls began to keep their distance, uncomfortable at her inappropriate behavior. Before the school year was over, Cammie, now totally addicted to bingeing and purging, had plunged into a deep depression.

"Everyone says I don't care about their feelings," Cammie said. "But how am I supposed to know what their feelings are? I try to be the way they want me to be, but then they want me to be someone totally different. I just don't get it."

Cammie didn't get it. With a father who was unemotional and uninvolved in her life, and a mother who was far more worried about how her daughter would reflect on her than about Cammie herself, the girl had never learned to process her own feelings, let alone those of others.

Now bulimic and addicted to alcohol, Cammie is getting therapy. Still her father won't come along for the family sessions. "I work hard every day," he says impatiently over the phone. "I just don't have the time." And how much does he earn from all his work? "About a million a year," he conceded. "It probably sounds like a lot, but it isn't enough. This family spends money like it's going out of style."

Cammie's story may not have a happy ending. Rejected by her father, she has a deep fear of intimacy, as do her mother and grandmother. She is trying to understand social dynamics and to learn new ways of coping. But the real problem is not her father's workaholism, or Cammie's alcoholism or bulimia. The real problem is the family secrets, which Cammie's father firmly refuses to acknowledge. "Everything is fine here," he insisted. "People look at us and admire us.

I'd dare say just about everyone in this city would love to trade places with us."

With an adolescent who is bulimic, there are often controlling parents. There is a lot of hidden guilt in the family, and there is a great deal of pressure to meet high family standards. Family therapy is vital. If the bulimia is brought under control but the other issues in the family are not confronted, the "recovered" bulimic may become involved in some other problem behavior such as shoplifting, drinking, smoking, or sexual addiction.

Bulimics share some or all of these common characteristics. They may:

- have a need to "feed" their emotional pain
- use the bingeing and purging to numb their pain in the same way drug addicts use drugs
- try to wrest some control for themselves, especially from their parents (This is true even when the parents themselves are totally out of control.)
- have a need to be perfect, to make all appear well on the outside
- tend to compensate for a parent being overweight
- are preoccupied with food
- are compulsive in other areas, such as work and school
- have suffered abuse, emotional, physical, or sexual

It used to be that bulimia and anorexia mainly affected young people. But now girls who have been affected since adolescence have grown up. Women who

suffered from these disorders in younger years may believe they have successfully conquered the problem. But
if the disorder has never been dealt with emotionally,
when a stressor hits they will be thrown right back into
that old anorexic or bulimic pattern. They may try to
keep it from their families, but this is seldom successful.
What they do succeed in is turning the eating disorder
into a family secret. As with other secrets, what is passed
on to their children is that the behavior is acceptable so
long as it is kept quiet.

Socioholic or Churchaholic

Everyone admired the Barbella family. If the
church doors were open, they were there, the first to
arrive and the last to leave. They knew everyone and
everyone knew them. Sounds like a good, healthy family, you say? Well, not exactly. The Barbellas are
"churchaholics."

At first glance, both socioholics and churchaholics
seem admirable. But consider the characteristics they
tend to share.

- They must be seen at the right places. (For the
  Barbellas, this was at church.)
- In their opinion, their lifestyle is the only right way
  to live, and anyone who doesn't follow it is wrong.
- They tend to be critical of anyone who is not in
  their circle.
- They are motivated not by a concern for others or

by a love for God, but by their own need to be
accepted.

- Their motivation comes from outward pressure
  rather than from inward peace.
- While they outwardly appear confident and secure,
  inside they are terribly insecure.
- They cannot say no for fear of rejection.
- Much like workaholics, they are addicted to staying
  busy.

Like other addictions, socioholics and churchaholics pass their disability on down through the generations. The children copy what their parents model. The
secret the next generation learns is *Happiness comes
from being with the "in crowd," whether socially or at
church*. As adults, some of the children tend to fall in
line and do likewise. Others become the opposite of
what they see in their parents, turning their backs on
the church or on other social contacts. Either way, the
children of the next generation often grow into adults
who lack balance in their lives.

Sexual Addictions

Marilyn's father has always given her the message
that girls aren't as important or as worthy as boys. Now
in her twenties, Marilyn has a desperate need to feel
close to a man, to be important to him. Unfortunately
she looks for value in the wrong way—she is addicted to
sex. Marilyn sleeps with man after man, searching des-

perately for that special one who will give her the sense of worthiness she never got from her father. But it is a vicious cycle. The more men Marilyn sleeps with, the more worthless she feels. The more worthless she feels, the more frantically she tries to find that right man.

Sexual addictions come in many forms, but at the center of each is the destruction of boundaries. A daughter needs intimacy from her father, but if sex becomes a barrier between them, she can no longer trust him. Once the relationship is broken, it is very difficult to repair, because the basic boundaries have been destroyed.

That's the real harm in sexual abuse. It has broken a trust that's irreplaceable. Because of that, it is probably the toughest of all addictions, and one of the hardest to forgive.

Whether the secret sexual addiction takes the form of lust, pornography, cross-dressing, prostitution, indiscriminate sex, incest, or sexual abuse, sexual addicts have the following characteristics in common.

- They treat individuals as if they were objects to be used rather than as people in their own rights.
- They have a distinct lack of feeling.
- They don't understand true intimacy.
- They never received the appropriate modeling that a healthy sexual relationship involves.

Sexual addictions, too, are passed along generationally. This happens in several ways. It happens through inappropriate sexual talk. It happens when there is nudity among family members when the children are at an age where they are sexually curious. It happens when the children are rigidly taught that sex is bad, a situation that causes the children to get hooked into sexual addictions as a way of breaking free from their family. It happens when the children are violated physically or sexually, or when they see their mother abused. It happens when sons see inappropriate modeling from their fathers—for instance, when a father who is into pornography shows no real intimacy toward his wife.

The results of sexual addictions are ugly and destructive. They cause irreparable emotional damage. They also cause great harm spiritually, for sexual sin makes it difficult to be close to God.

Obsessive-Compulsive Behavior

Remember the story in Luke 10:38–42 about Jesus' visit with his friends Mary and Martha? Mary so enjoyed her relationship with Jesus that she spent the time sitting at His feet, hanging on His every word. Not Martha. She was so caught up in the business of entertaining that she had no time to sit and listen to Jesus. What's more, it made her angry to see Mary sitting there while she was doing all the work.

"Jesus," Martha said, "tell Mary to get up and give me some help."

But instead of scolding Mary, Jesus told Martha she needed to reevaluate her priorities. Martha was an obsessive-compulsive person who had to be continually performing to feel worthy.

What causes a person to be obsessive-compulsive? Certainly it can begin with what a child sees modeled by his parents—for instance, a parent may have rituals for cleaning up or washing her hands that the child observes. Children are influenced by parents who have to have everything in perfect order, or parents who insist, "Do it my way or else!"

Obsessive-compulsive behavior, too, is passed along generationally. Some children become just like their parents. It's almost as if there were an internal parent telling the adult child he is worthless unless he does things the way Mom and Dad said they should be done. Others rebel against the behavior of their overly rigid parents and become the opposite, growing up to be lazy or messy or chronically late. For still others, obsessive thoughts and compulsive behavior become a way to control the pain within themselves, and, in time, it becomes a way of controlling their own children.

Gambling

Fred Watson was the everyday-type guy you can find sitting in the same church pew every Sunday. He was an upstanding man who would not be caught dead in a bar.

Even though Fred was struggling financially in his business, his wife and family spent more and more money. Feeling terribly inadequate as a provider for his family, he was consumed by his efforts to search out money-raising schemes. Gambling, he decided, would offer him the best chance to get the most money in the shortest amount of time. First it was just friendly card games, then it got more and more serious until Fred totally lost control. "I was certain I could beat the system," Fred later admitted. "My winnings were going to be the answer to all my problems."

But Fred didn't beat the system. Instead he became ever more hopelessly mired in debt. Yet the more his indebtedness grew, the more obsessed he became with winning.

Fred was such a good liar that his wife never suspected a thing until two men showed up at the house to collect his debts and ended up roughing him up. Then his secret was out, and everything came tumbling down around him.

By the time Fred sought counseling, he had lost his business and was thousands of dollars in debt to loan sharks.

Gamblers are always trying to get rich quick. They see an easy way to get money without having to work and save and wait. Sure, they know lots of others are trying to win, but they are certain that they can beat the system. To them, winning means success, a chance to prove just how good they are. It is the ultimate challenge.

Anyone lured into the pot-of-gold-at-the-end-of-the-rainbow illusion of gambling would do well to remember the words of Ecclesiastes 5:10: "He who loves silver will not be satisfied with silver; Nor he who loves abundance, with increase. This also is vanity."

Few gamblers are winners. And even those who do win are seldom satisfied with their gain.

Addictions Are Passed Along

"It's not a generational thing," Cammie's mother insisted of her daughter's bulimia and alcohol abuse. "No one in either my family or my husband's has ever had such problems."

In their family the specific crisis of bulimia was new, but as we have seen again and again, family secrets do tend to be generational. Even though the form of the addiction changes, the secret remains, and the power of that secret moves on from generation to generation to generation. Imagine the scenario of a person carrying a big sack of rocks—his burdens. The bag is heavy, but he can handle it. The struggle continues because he has never learned from his family how to relieve himself of those burdens in an emotionally healthy way. Then comes the day when one last rock is added to the load, and suddenly the whole load comes crashing down.

Addictions can be passed on to the next generation either actively or passively. Passing addictions *actively* means that adult children follow their parents' modeling. Passing them *passively* has to do with the secretive giving of permission.

Passing Addictions Actively

Words can harm, and even destroy, children. It is indeed unfortunate that so many parents seem unable to understand this. What parents say and do greatly affects how their children think and what they become. Parents' words and actions have an enormous impact on what patterns their children will adopt and carry on into their adult relationships, and in time will pass on to their own children.

As we have seen, adult children sometimes do just the opposite of what their parents do. The son of an alcoholic may not touch a drop of alcohol, but he eats only health food and is a faithful marathon runner. All of the son's choices are potentially good and healthy—*if* he is able to pursue them in moderation. That's an important *if*. Healthy families are balanced, but unhealthy ones tend to swing from one dysfunctional pattern to another—from one end of the continuum to the other.

Passing Addictions Passively

To be passive means to give permission. A father who sexually abuses his daughter sends the message to his son that this is acceptable behavior. So what does the son do? He abuses his own daughter. The abused daughter gets a message, too: "This is the way females are treated." So what does she do? She marries a man who abuses their daughters.

Sometimes adult children think they are taking a

step in the right direction by focusing on their parents' addiction. But understanding the problem doesn't help unless they get to the root cause.

Chapter 3 talked about admitting the secret and stepping out to be a secret-breaker. But the cycle cannot be broken simply by talking about the problem. The secret is much too strong for that. The only answer is to get to the base of the problem, and from there to work toward bringing about healing.

Overcoming Addiction Secrets

For those who recognize—or even suspect—addiction secrets in the family, there are ten suggestions to help.

1. *Explore the family history.* Ask questions about problems among the relatives. But be aware that family members might gloss over hidden addictions. Of Grandpa Joe's alcoholism they might say, "Oh, well, I guess he did hit the bottle a little."

2. *Look through the denial.* Secrets are by nature clouded by denial. Look deeply for the truth. Talk to people who know and care about you, who can help you see yourself objectively.

3. *Look for patterns.* Are there personal patterns that mirror other family members' addictions? (If spending money is a struggle and someone says,

"You shop just like Aunt Sue!" it may be a clue to take the matter seriously.) If a family member is addicted, seek professional advice about the best way to help.

4. *Admit your own addictions*—a difficult but vital step.

5. *Seek professional help.* Professional help can assist in recognizing the family pain that started the addiction. Counseling can help stop both the addiction and the addictive pattern.

6. *Find an accountability partner.* In recovering from a secret addiction, there is a need for someone to confide in, someone to give spiritual guidance and support. This is also helpful when it is a family member who is recovering.

7. *Attend support groups.* Support groups are a safe place to make the secret known, thereby robbing it of its power. The group can also help maintain your healing and provide an atmosphere to discuss the affects of a family member's addiction.

8. *Look for ways to change your behavior toward the children.* This step can have the greatest effect on changing personal behavior. If behaviors surface that could develop into a full blown addiction, or if a child is already addicted, ask for a professional evaluation.

9. *Commit to daily prayer and Scripture meditation.*

This will go a long way toward keeping you free from addictions and secrets. Pray for the children as they are educated about any family addictions, and commit to serve as a role model for them. Renewing your mind daily through the Scriptures is the only way to overcome an addiction.

10. *Accept the significance of the story of Jesus Christ.* His story is one of healing, grace, peace, and for-giveness.

5

Financial Secrets

The Schaffers had a financial secret.

"We had a bunch of little debts that somehow just grew and grew," Darlene Schaffer said. "We felt we had no choice but to borrow fifteen thousand dollars so we could pay them all off."

The problem was, the Schaffers kept on using their credit cards. Before long, their debts were right back up there, only now they owed the fifteen-thousand-dollar consolidation loan as well. "We were worse off than ever!" Darlene cried. "We had no choice but to declare bankruptcy."

That was five years ago, and guess what? The Schaffers are in the same cycle all over again. In tears, Darlene said, "We're going back to bankruptcy court next week. I just can't believe we have made such a mess of our finances. I really can't believe we've done it twice!"

Unfortunately, the Schaffers are not that unusual. Some families repeat this cycle over and over and over again.

There are people who intentionally take on financial secrets. Margaret uses her secret to punish her husband. Whenever they have a fight, she goes on a shopping spree. It's her way of saying, "That will teach you!"

Linda doesn't argue with her family. Whenever she feels wronged, she simply spends money. Her message is: "You owe me this!"

Whatever their rationale, people who overspend all end up the same place: in financial trouble.

Seven Common Financial Secrets

Financial Secret 1: Drowning in Debt

How do uncontrollable debts occur? Here are a few explanations people give:

- "I knew we were overspending, but we had to. We had to keep up appearances in front of the neighbors/our friends/her family/my family."
- "Everyone else had a boat, so we needed to get one too."
- "We just couldn't stretch our money far enough to pay all our bills, so we got farther and farther behind."
- "Our house was repossessed, but we told everyone we sold it."
- "Every time creditors called, we told them the check was in the mail."

- "Life has never been fair to me. I spend because now it's my turn to have some special things in life."
- "My father was such a selfish old skinflint. I always swore when I grew up I'd have all the things everyone else has, and now I do."

Although these explanations may not seem logical, for many people they tell the whole story—many people like Nancy and Jack.

Even though they are deeply mired in debt, Nancy and Jack wear expensive clothes, drive new cars, and have their children in private school. "I just don't see how we can cut back," Nancy earnestly told us. The clothes? "They are important!" she insisted. "If we don't look nice, we won't feel good about ourselves. And if we don't feel good about who we are, we won't get anywhere in life." The new cars? "They are no better than what all our friends drive." Private school? "Oh, we couldn't give that up. Both of our families think that private schools are important."

Everyone likes nice things. But some people are especially driven to spend way beyond their means. Both Nancy and Jack grew up in families that didn't believe in delaying gratification. If they wanted something, they got it, and they got it now. And Nancy and Jack wanted a lot of things.

In Romans 13:8 the apostle Paul writes: "Owe no one anything except to love one another, for he who loves another has fulfilled the law." This is excellent advice for all of us, especially those of us struggling with debts.

Financial Secret 2: Bankruptcy

Bankruptcy is an area that can easily become a family secret. When little Johnny asks, "Daddy, why are those men taking our car?" Daddy answers, "Oh, we decided to get rid of it." If Johnny persists with something like, "Why? Are we getting a new one?" Daddy keeps the deception going by answering, "No, we just decided we didn't need that car."

Certainly bankruptcy is a private issue. There is no reason to broadcast it to everyone. But when people have to lie to their own family members to hide the situation, what began as a financial problem becomes rooted as a family secret. Keeping a bankruptcy too closely guarded a secret can cause a person to lose the support, both emotional and practical, that those close to him would have been able to give.

Even when the bankruptcy is not their fault, families can be devastated. The Bennet family had always been careful with their money, but when Tom had a heart attack that required surgery not covered by their insurance, the family was forced into bankruptcy. Tom Bennet keeps this secret from his parents. "How can I tell them?" he asked. "It is the most humiliating thing that has ever happened to me."

None of us can foresee unexpected disasters that can wipe out our financial reserves. For those in bankruptcy, the Scripture has words of hope. "Though he fall, he shall not be utterly cast down; for the LORD upholds him with His hand" (Ps. 37:24). With the assurance that God has not forsaken you, even bankruptcy does not have to become a family secret.

Financial Secret 3: Inheritance

For some people, an inheritance is a wonderful blessing that eases financial pressures and opens up wonderful possibilities for the family, and even beyond. For others, it is the doorway to fighting, pain, and new family secrets.

"My whole life, my mother controlled us kids by threatening to cut us out of her will," one man told us. "After she died, we found that she had never even written a will."

Blended families are a common breeding ground for secrets. After the divorce and remarriage, Dad cuts his first children out of his will—a devastating rejection for the kids. The children's mother, weary from always trying to get money out of her ex-husband, looks in exasperation at the comparatively comfortable circumstances of his new family and tells her kids, "Look what your dad did for those kids. He never did anything like that for you!" So the kids figure, "If Dad really loved me, he would at least have left me money."

Usually, parents are partial to their own children. But where secrets are concerned, there are all kinds of exceptions. Cindy represents one.

Soon after Cindy's parents divorced, her mom remarried. When her mother gave birth to identical twin boys, Cindy was basically written out of the family. She looked like her natural father which earned her even fewer points. The twins were dressed in expensive clothes and they played with the hottest toys on the market. Cindy made do with leftovers and hand-me-downs. The final rejection: no inheritance. Her secret conviction was *I don't belong.*

Greg and Randy represent another exception. Greg's father was a super jock, while Greg was what could best be described as a computer nut. Stepson Randy, however, was a sports lover and a great player of every game that came along. What did this father do? He ignored his biological son and fawned over his stepson, whom he described as "a real man's man." You can guess who fared best in this father's will.

The greatest inheritance problems usually occur in families where the children never felt that they received enough of their parents' time, attention, and love. To make up for what they missed back then, the children fight over the smallest things in their parents' wills. One young woman battled her sister over their mother's comb and brush set. Why? Because each young woman was desperate to have a "part of Mom" all her own. In loving, healthy families, the greatest inheritance is not monetary; it is love, acceptance, shared values, faith in God, and warm memories.

Financial Secret 4: Not Paying Taxes

It's amazing how many people have secrets involving the payment of taxes. "I couldn't pay!" Dwayne

Favor insisted. "I didn't have the money." He didn't mention the new car he had just bought or the expensive cruise his family took.

"So I wasn't totally honest on my income tax return," said Meg Franklin. "Who is?"

"I didn't cheat. I reported my income," Allen Delgado argued when his wife insisted he come in for counseling. That extra income he earned "under the table"? "Oh, that," Allen said with a shrug. "There's nothing wrong with that. Everyone does it."

"I'm in big trouble for not filing my income taxes," said James Lombardi. "Well, I don't think I should have to pay. No one asks me if I want to finance all that government waste. Well, I don't want to. And I don't intend to."

A common family tax secret works this way: For years Dad has been cheating on his taxes and has never been caught. Then his son takes his father's financial manipulation a step or two further, and he *is* caught. "What?" the son exclaims in honest dismay. "What's going on? We've been doing this for years, and there has never been a problem."

But the secret doesn't stop there. The son's boy carries it on into the next generation by cheating in school. "Well," the youngster exclaims when he is caught, "you cheat on your taxes. What's the difference?"

Again, we see that old law of reaping greater than what is sown. A father puts a little extra weight on the scales when he weighs the meat in his family butcher shop; his son cheats on his taxes; his grandson embez-zles at the bank. "How could he ever have done that?" the perplexed family asks. How? By copying the atti-tudes and actions he saw modeled by his father and grandfather. It is the family secret that gives the young man family permission.

Some people lead such dysfunctional and unorga-nized lives that they just can't get it together to pay their taxes. Then they become so fearful and worried that they are less functional than ever. The secret turns into a self-fulfilling prophecy: "See? I *am* a failure at everything I do. I can't even pay my taxes!"

It is clear from Scripture that God intends us to meet our civil obligations. Romans 13:6–7 says, "For because of this you also pay taxes, for they are God's ministers attending continually to this very thing. Render therefore to all their due: taxes to whom taxes are due, customs to whom customs, fear to whom fear, honor to whom honor."

Financial Secret 5: Financial Lies

Clinton Browning grew up extremely poor. So fearful was he of dying in poverty that he held tightly to every dollar he got his hands on. No one would guess he was a multimillionaire. He gave very little to others, for he was truly afraid he wouldn't have enough left for himself. And he married a woman who was just like him.

A good deal of the family's food came from the large garden Clinton's wife kept, and the cattle and chickens she and Clinton raised. They saved rubber bands, they washed and reused plastic bags, they saved glass jars for canning, and they never threw an article of clothing away.

The Browning's son, Doug, grew to be just like his parents. He staunchly refused to spend money on family vacations, or even on baby-sitters so that he and his wife could get out alone once in a while. His response was always the same: "If we spend our money now, we will be sorry. What will we do on a rainy day?"

Doug's daughter, Sarah, is newly married. She feels the deprivation of her younger years so acutely that she spends money frivolously. Not long ago she saw some shoes she liked, so she bought a pair in every color—and a purse to go with every pair. "I am never going to be like my penny-pinching family!" she swore. Instead she is rapidly becoming a shopaholic and heading for bankruptcy.

All three generations of the Browning family share a common secret: Rather than controlling money, they allow money to control them.

Most financial lies occur when one spouse lies to another. The lies may be about how much money is being spent and what it is being spent on. It may be about how much money a spouse has. It may be hoarded money the spouse knows nothing about. It may be the hidden true price of something, or extra credit cards the other isn't aware of, or secret bank accounts. Or the lie may be about unpaid bills.

Healthy families don't need to lie to each other.

Financial Secret 6: Gifts

Betty Jean gave to everyone for every occasion.

"You overdo it," her husband said.

"But giving is good!" Betty Jean countered. "The Bible even tells us that it is more blessed to give than to receive."

Betty Jean is right, of course. But the issue is, What is her reason for all that giving?

Some people give for the purpose of having others see their generosity. The goal is to gain status. Others give money privately, but for the wrong reasons—such as to fulfill a legalistic obligation. ("If I don't give, God will punish me.")

Another side to secrets of giving is manipulation. Many people attempt to bribe God. "If I give to God, I know He will give me back a hundredfold," they say. The implication is that if they give, God *has* to give back to them. This idea is even preached from many pulpits. But what happens when a person gives and gives and gives, Sunday after Sunday, and never gets anything back? It's easy for that person to get angry at God. "How come the windows of heaven haven't opened over me yet?" he asks. "When is my payoff coming? I've invested an awful lot over the years, and God owes me."

In 2 Corinthians 9:7, we are told precisely how we are to give: "So let each one give as he purposes in his heart, not grudgingly or of necessity; for God loves a cheerful giver." The correct approach is to give responsibly for the glory of God, out of a thankful and grateful heart, with no strings attached.

Financial Secret 7: Financial Dreams

Everyone in the Randolph family is either a medical doctor or has a Ph.D. It is an unspoken expectation of the family, ingrained in the children from an early age.

Son Brian, at age twenty-two, is bright and capable, but very unhappy. "I have no idea why I'm in medical school!" he says bitterly. "I don't even want to be a doctor."

Brian is filling his family's need for status—most unhappily.

Status, and the role a person is expected to fill in society, passes along from generation to generation.

Families can hardly help but pass their financial dreams along to their children. Whether the unspoken message is, "Be like me. Make money and I will be proud of you," or "Don't be like me. Be the success I never was, and then I will be proud of you," it comes through loud and clear.

Joe couldn't miss the message from his family. His parents never had much in the way of material goods, but Joe was a bright boy, and his parents had great hopes and dreams for his success. With their encouragement, he won a full scholarship for college and then another one for law school. Joe went on to become a high-powered attorney with a driving ambition to earn more and more money. It was only when his wife took their children and left him that he began to understand the price he was paying to make his father's financial dreams for him come true.

It's too bad Joe and his family did not recognize the truth of Christ's words in Matthew 6:21: "For where your treasure is, there your heart will be also."

Why Do Families Keep Financial Secrets?

There are several reasons for financial secrets. One of the most relentless is the quest for power.

Quest for Power

There are some people who have an overwhelming need to control the things around them, and being in control of the finances gives them the feeling of power they crave. Others are convinced that money and the things it will buy will ensure the security and happiness they long for. Still others see spending money as a good way to control love. They don't have to demonstrate true intimacy but can command love if they can shower their family and friends with gifts.

Helen's father seldom spent time with his children, and he never told them he loved them. The way he earned his place in their affections was by giving them things. Now in her early thirties, Helen still equates spending with love. But Helen's husband Chris doesn't earn the kind of money her dad did, and it is causing major problems in their marriage.

"Helen spends and spends on the children, even

though she knows we can't afford it," Chris says. "Everything those kids want, they get."

"Chris just doesn't love the children as much as I do," Helen insists. "He says he does, but if he did he wouldn't be so miserly with them!"

As for the children, they are growing up confused about money and at the center of a power struggle.

Quest for Success

Families that keep financial secrets in a quest for success believe they have to have more and more material goods in order to feel good about themselves. Karen is a good example of this thinking.

"I was deprived as a child," Karen said. "My father was the pastor of a small church that paid him next to nothing. All through high school and college, I was acutely aware of my out-of-fashion second-hand clothes, donated by the congregation."

Then she married Robert. Robert was extremely successful in his family's business, and, knowing of his wife's deprived background, he encouraged her to spend money. And spend she did. "I admit my closet is stuffed with more clothes than I could wear out in three lifetimes," Karen says, "but after growing up the way I did, it feels so good to have all the stylish clothes I want. Even if I never wear them, just seeing them hanging in my closet makes me feel like I'm somebody."

Karen's fifteen-year-old daughter knows nothing about struggling financially. And when Karen tells her about her old friends who liked her regardless of the clothes she wore, the fashion-conscious teenager can't understand. Her secret is she is convinced that unless a person has a lot of great clothes, no one will want to be caught dead with her.

Quest for Status

Many, many families who keep financial secrets do so because of their quest for status in the community. They have to shop at the right stores; they must be seen in the right places; they are required to drive the right cars. They have to belong to the right organizations and clubs, to live in the right neighborhoods, to eat in the right restaurants. Their children must attend the right schools, and then the right universities. Their lives are centered around "keeping up with the Joneses," or better yet, zipping way ahead of them.

Fear

Other people are driven to financial secrets by their fears. Sometimes the fear is realistic and sometimes it is not.

Realistic Fear

"We have to save money!" Whether the fear is still appropriate or not, people who grew up poor have this old tape playing over and over and over again inside their heads.

One man's big secret was that his family lost all their money when the real estate market crashed. He grasps and hoards his money because of an old realistic fear from his past. The hoarding is no longer necessary, but the old tapes are still playing loud and clear. This secret is creating tremendous problems in that man's family.

Another realistic fear is that someone will abuse money because it actually happened in the past. One woman came into her marriage financially irresponsible. After a few years, she stopped her spending sprees, but that old tension and fear remain. Although no one ever talks about it, she is not given access to credit cards or the checkbook, and she has to ask for and account for every dime she spends. Her husband simply will not allow her to change.

Another realistic fear is the poverty of widowhood. Barbara, in her mid-thirties, is single. "I'm not getting any younger," she frets. "What's going to happen to me when I get old? I won't have enough money to take care of myself." She remembers the grandmother who had to come to live with her family because she had no money. Barbara's fear of being poverty-stricken in her old age is so acute that it is robbing her of the joy of living now.

Philippians 4:19 can be a real help in the face of real fears: "And my God shall supply all your need according to His riches in glory by Christ Jesus."

Unrealistic Fear

Some fears are not founded in reality; among them the behavior of hoarding. Lucille is a good example of a hoarder.

Lucille goes into a store for a quart of milk and a loaf of bread and comes out with fifty dollars worth of groceries she doesn't need. "But these things are all on sale!" she says. If she buys something and later finds the item on sale for less, it just about drives her crazy. Her pantry is so stuffed with food that much of it spoils before she and her husband can eat it. Her house— every drawer, every shelf, every closet, every corner— bulges with junk she has picked up at garage sales. "It was such a good deal," she explains. "I just couldn't pass it up."

Another unrealistic fear is related to the quest for success: If you don't have enough money, or the right house, or enough material possessions, happiness is impossible. People with this fear are forever striving to get to the place where they can finally say, "Now my family will be okay." There is great power in this secret, but absolutely no truth.

Still another unrealistic fear is that we are destined by fate to repeat the mistakes of our families.

"The men in my family always make bad investments, and look what I just did," Patrick said, detailing an impulsive business move. When asked why he made such a decision in the first place, Patrick replied, "I just had a feeling."

"That feeling" may be simply the habit of old familiar family patterns. When urged to think his moves through on a rational, intelligent level, Patrick began to make much wiser decisions. He realized he is not destined to repeat his family's mistakes.

Pride Before a Fall

Pride propels many families into financial secrets. "We just couldn't ask for help," they say. Or, "I have to be independent." Or, "I don't want everyone to see me as a failure."

When a family has lost—or in some cases has squandered—money, their pride keeps them from being honest about what happened. This was the case with Doreen and her husband. When Doreen's parents sold their ranch, they took the huge profit and divided it up among their four children. It came out to almost half a million dollars each. While Doreen's two brothers and one sister put their money in the bank or in mutual funds, Doreen and her husband used theirs to fulfill a life-long dream. They bought a small business.

Although Doreen and her husband worked day and night, they simply did not know enough about running such an enterprise, and within two years, the business failed. "I couldn't tell my parents what happened," Doreen said. "They would be so angry." So for several years she and her husband hid the business failure. When it finally came to light, they lied about how it had happened: "It was really unfortunate timing. Every business that started up that year failed."

Men are especially prone to feel like terrible failures. The fact of the matter is that in any investment, there is always the possibility of losing. A functional family is able to work through such a loss and the disappointment it brings. It is the unspoken messages that can generate a family secret. The message from Doreen's family was, "We're giving you this money, but you have to use it the way we want you to. And you'd better not lose it!" But because the message was unspoken, Doreen never had any real guidelines, nor was she able to discuss the boundaries with her parents.

Pride and keeping secrets is never God's way. Proverbs 16:18 warns, "Pride goes before destruction, and a haughty spirit before a fall."

Secrets as Punishment and Revenge

Money is often used—quite effectively—as punishment and revenge. People punish by spending as well as by withholding money. Each of these approaches pushes the other partner into the role of child, a tactic that inevitably produces a great deal of anger.

Ronald and Gloria had very serious problems in their marriage. Ronald's father had always controlled the money in his family. He had paid all the bills and had given Ronald's mother an allowance. The secret belief in Ronald's family is *Women can't be trusted with money and need to be controlled.* When Ronald married Gloria, he tried to establish the same system, but with very different results.

"Gloria insisted on having her own checking account," Ronald said. "She deposited her paycheck in that account and she paid her own bills from it. Now I ask you, what kind of a system is that for a married couple?"

Now that Gloria has quit work and is at home full time with their new baby, Ronald is punishing her former independence by withholding money from her and making her ask for everything she needs.

"I can't even buy fingernail polish or go out to lunch with my friends," Gloria said. "I can't buy diapers for the baby without asking him!"

It took a good bit of counseling for Ronald to be able to see the root of their problem: He was angry because Gloria didn't want to handle money the way his family had always done. Even then, it wasn't until Gloria threatened to take the baby and leave that he finally agreed to discuss alternative ways of handling family finances. In many cases, the secret is subtle. In Ronald's family, his father said he took care of the money because he was good at it; actually it was his way to control Ronald's mother. When Gloria didn't let Ronald control her, he grew angry and tried to do it by withholding cash.

Secrets of Dishonesty

Leland considered himself a good and honest man. Yet when the opportunity presented itself to make a few extra charges on his company's expense report, it made perfect sense to him to seize the moment. "What's so bad about that?" Leland asked in complete sincerity. "It's what is called doing business American style."

Caroline, too, saw no dishonesty in what she was doing. Although she always helped herself to things at work—just little things such as envelopes and stamps, pencils and marking pens for her children—she insisted she was justified because "I'm not paid that well. That company owes me." But when the principal at school called to tell her that her nine-year-old daughter was caught taking money out of her teacher's desk, Caroline was horrified. "My daughter is a thief!" she exclaimed. "I can't understand it. She knows it's wrong to steal."

Dishonesty can be insidious. If an activity must be rationalized, hidden, or justified, the line has almost certainly been crossed into secret-keeping. Consider the apostle Paul's words in Acts 24:16: "This being so, I myself always strive to have a conscience without offense toward God and men."

Secrets of Envy and Greed

The two vices of envy and greed have tricked many unsuspecting people into secret-keeping. Even so, it is difficult for people to see and admit what is actually driving them.

Reverend Von Rentzel, his wife, and their three children, lived happy but frugal lives. Once the children were grown and Reverend Von Rentzel had retired from the ministry, he made a shocking announcement to his family: He was a millionaire several times over, with investments and landholdings throughout the world.

"Why didn't you ever tell us?" his older daughter demanded.

"Because I was afraid of what it might do to you children and to the people in the church," her father replied. "You might have become haughty or greedy. And members of the congregation might have been envious. I decided that if no one knew, no one would be hurt."

After the shock wore off, Reverend Von Rentzel's son looked his father straight in the eye and said, "I can't help but wonder, Dad, what other secrets have you been keeping from us?" Von Rentzel's fear of others' envy caused him to keep his secret.

Even "good" secrets can build up a great deal of resentment, suspicion, and distrust in a family. "He was far more concerned about appearances than he was about the work of God," his daughter said.

His son added, "We had to do without so many things, and there really was no reason for it. Dad had no right to do that to us."

This father's motive was good, but he could have handled the matter in a better way. For instance, he might have told his family, "We have this money, but we don't need it now, so we're going to put it in a trust for you for the future." The kids might not have agreed with him, but they would have known he was being honest with them.

Even when the intentions are laudable, the dynamics of secrets are surprisingly powerful. Even "good" secrets can lead to problems.

The Cost of Financial Secrets

In the second chapter of Ecclesiastes, King Solomon talks about getting everything he wanted. "Whatever my eyes desired I did not keep from them. I did not withhold my heart from any pleasure" (Eccl. 2:10). Yet even all the wealth and pleasure the world could give Solomon did not satisfy him. In verse 11 he goes on to state, "Then I looked on all the works that my hands had done and on the labor in which I had toiled; and indeed all was vanity and grasping for the wind."

After tasting all the pleasures that money could buy, King Solomon finally came to realize the pursuit was no more successful than grasping for the wind. There was no satisfaction in it.

Material goods often fail to bring the pleasure they promise. Moreover, keeping financial secrets comes at an extremely high cost. Physically, financial secrets rob families of financial security, relationships, and a true sense of worth. Emotionally, financial secrets create constant stress, putting a terrible strain on marriage and family relationships and destroying intimacy and trust.

But most significantly, financial secrets create huge walls between families and God. Most keepers of financial secrets elevate money to the place where God should rightfully be. For many, the spiritual toll comes when everything falls apart, and in bitterness they turn their blame toward God. "Why did you let it happen?" they cry. "You should have protected me!"

God allows us to suffer the consequences of our actions, but it is a hard lesson.

Perhaps it is to protect us from this spiritual toll that we are instructed in Hebrews 13:5: "Let your conduct be without covetousness; be content with such things as you have. For He Himself has said, 'I will never leave you nor forsake you.' "

Even in the wake of devastating financial secrets, God is there to offer help and healing.

Healing After the Secrets

Healing in the aftermath of financial secrets comes in all three areas in which family members have had to pay: emotional, physical, and spiritual.

Emotional Healing

In order to heal emotionally, a family needs to talk openly, to share honestly, to be willing to be real before one another. It's not enough to talk around the surface of the issue. It is important to dig to the roots, so that family members understand the underlying dynamics and just what it is that needs to be resolved. Only then can a family move on to the next step of reestablishing trust.

Certainly trust is never reestablished without honest sharing and a good deal of talking. Commitments and promises to a spouse and children are important. Yet words alone are not enough. Reestablishing trust also requires actions. Those commitments have to be lived up to. Those promises must be fulfilled. Talk must be followed by action.

Physical Healing

Physical healing in this case means achieving financial health. This begins with learning to live on the existing income. Impossible? Don't be too quick to surrender. Healing begins by making out a realistic family budget. (There are many helpful financial planning books on the market. If more help is needed than what you can get from books, find a financial planner or some other expert who can assist you.) Let this be a family project. A family that has worked together to decide where and how the money should be spent is far more likely to stick to that budget.

Financial healing should include a savings plan. It is important to anticipate upcoming expenditures—a new car, college, the family vacation, retirement. Saving ahead for these things will prevent throwing the family back into the old financial problems that foster secrets.

In Luke 14:28, Jesus said, "For which of you, intending to build a tower, does not sit down first and count the cost, whether he has enough to finish it." When it comes to deciding where and how to spend money, make this the cornerstone.

Spiritual Healing

The journey toward spiritual healing begins by giving to the Lord. Although tithing is not a commandment in the New Testament, giving a good percentage of the family income to God right off the top is a good way to get into the habit of giving to the Lord.

If the response is, "Why should I give to God? He hasn't come through for me. Look at how I have to struggle financially"—this is a sure sign of unresolved bitterness toward God. Cut those strings that are attached to your gifts to Him and turn to Him in trust.

If the response is, "I don't think God will want my gifts now. My attitude hasn't been very good"—this is a sure sign of unresolved forgiveness.

Part of spiritual healing is forgiving yourself for the past and forgiving other people for how they have treated you. Offering forgiveness is in itself a gift to God.

Another step in spiritual healing is wise stewardship of the assets God has entrusted to you. Most of us approach money as something we earn, and therefore something that is rightfully ours. But the truth is, everything we have belongs to God. Timothy warned the early Christians: "Command those who are rich in this present age not to be haughty, nor to trust in uncertain riches but in the living God, who gives us richly all things to enjoy" (1 Tim. 6:17). God allows us to be caretakers for His riches, as we learn in the parable of the talents (see Matt. 25:14–30). We have a duty to use what we have in a responsible manner, understanding that God has a perfect right to take back what He has entrusted to us.

Matthew 6:33 gives this perspective to follow:

"But seek first the kingdom of God and His righteousness, and all these things shall be added to you."

It is God's will that we use the wealth He gives us wisely and for His glory. He wants us to be appreciative and balanced in our lives. But above all He wants us to place our trust in Him, not in the wealth of the world. Only when we change our attitude about our assets—accepting them gratefully, being honest and asking forgiveness for our mistakes, and prayerfully seek to change—will there be no need for financial secrets.

6

Abuse Secrets

As a child, Priscilla had endured harsh whippings whenever she broke one of her father's many rules—and sometimes even when she didn't. One time after her father had whipped her for something her sister had done, he told her, "Just consider that for the times you've done wrong and I didn't catch you."

As a wife and mother, everyone considered Priscilla next-to-perfect. For years she faithfully taught the kindergarten Sunday school class, she was an active member of the P.T.A. the entire time her children were in school, and she gave truly inspired birthday parties for her kids.

The secret was that Priscilla hid her anger so well that only her family really knew what she was like. Only they endured the tirades over a schoolbook left on the table or a jacket not hung up. Only they experienced her scathing rage when someone was late for supper, or when a room wasn't cleaned properly or a grade wasn't up to par. Priscilla approached her family—especially her children—with constant angry demands for perfection.

When Priscilla finally came in for counseling, it was because of her grown children. "I don't understand them," she said. "My son is always angry. You know, he has actually hit his wife! And my daughter is cold and distant toward her husband and insists she never wants to have children. She says they are too messy and would spoil her and her husband's life. What's wrong with those kids of mine?"

What's wrong? Priscilla is seeing the results of children who have been raised with abuse. "Abuse!" she exclaimed at the suggestion. "Me? I never once hit my children. *I* was the one who was abused!"

While physical abuse is pretty easy to identify, emotional abuse—the most common type of battering —is much harder to define.

What Is Emotional Abuse?

There are three basic styles of emotional abuse: inappropriate anger, the lack of appropriate emotions, and the use of overwhelming emotions. Emotional abuse is hidden from outsiders; the emotional abuser keeps the secret by denying that he is really abusive. Abuse causes shame, which breeds secrets.

Inappropriate Anger

Priscilla is a good example of someone who abused with inappropriate anger. A family with this dysfunction often looks great on the outside. But what can't be readily seen is that at least one of the parents is filled with so much pent-up rage that it permeates every one of that person's relationships. Like the rageaholic in Chapter 4, every emotion he or she experiences—hurt, pain, fear, grief, loss—generates anger.

Lack of Appropriate Emotions

Children who suffer this type of emotional abuse are not allowed to express their emotions. "Big boys don't cry," they are scolded at the first sign of a tear. Or when they are angry, "Don't speak in that angry voice to me!" They are expected to experience all of life's events, including pain, grief, and loss, without showing emotion. Often children abused in this way grow into adults who simply don't know how to feel, and so they find it extremely difficult to have satisfying relationships with their spouses or children. Anytime the healthy expression of emotions is suppressed, this becomes a secret to the individual. Those who don't express their emotions may not even be sure what they are feeling at times.

Use of Overwhelming Emotions

This very common type of abuse has to do with the parents' piling their concerns and problems onto their children's little shoulders. Some adults keep their problems hidden from other adults who could help them. The child takes care of the parent instead of the parent caring for the child. In clinical circles this is referred to as "emotional incest." It simply means thrusting a child into an adult role. Whether the role is that of caretaker, breadwinner, disciplinarian, counselor, mediator, or even listener, it means forcing the child to carry a responsibility that is beyond the child's years.

Sometimes this "emotional incest" can be carried to an amazing extreme. Rachel and Sam had almost no emotional or physical intimacy in their marriage. In her loneliness, Rachel turned to her thirteen-year-old son, David, and focused all her time and attention on him. She told the boy about her arguments with his father, and detailed the problems between the two of them. Sam, too, confided in his son. He complained to him about how terribly difficult it was to live with Rachel. For days at a time Rachel and Sam refused to speak to each other. All of their communication went through David.

"Tell your mother I'm hungry and I want dinner," Sam would say.

"Tell your father he can fix his own dinner," Rachel would reply.

David was more like a marriage counselor, a struggling peacemaker, and a go-between than an adolescent just entering his teen years. "I think my parents are going to get a divorce, and it's all my fault," David told his counselor at school. "I have to do something, but I don't know what."

When Rachel and Sam were referred for counseling, neither one could comprehend how anyone could possibly say they were subjecting their son to emotional abuse. "The one thing we agree on is that we both love David," Rachel said.

Sam added, "We are lucky to have a son who is so mature. He is a great kid—obviously very well-adjusted."

Emotionally Abusive Behaviors

Like Rachel and Sam, who both care a great deal about their son, most parents do not intentionally set out to harm their children. They just are not able to see their behavior as emotional abuse.

So what behaviors actually are emotionally abusive, to children or to other adults?

Pouting

Pouting is the "feel sorry for me" syndrome. Ted was a master at this abusive technique.

Because of the marriage problems Valerie and Ted were having, Valerie wanted the two of them to go for counseling together. Since they had already planned to have a nice dinner out, Valerie decided that a pleasant setting like that would be a good time to approach Ted with her idea.

Ted didn't like the idea at all. At the first mention of seeing a counselor, he stopped eating, stopped talking, and pouted through the rest of the dinner. All evening he was angry, and when they got up the next morning, he was still pouting. "All right," Valerie finally told him. "I'll forget the whole idea."

Manipulation

Manipulation can take many forms. Charles manipulated his son, Evan, with guilt. "You have got to make good grades in school. Your mother worries when you don't do well, and the worry is making her sick."

Today, Evan is a minister who demands that his family project a certain image. He didn't want his six-teen-year-old daughter, Chrissy, to be on the school cheerleading squad because "It wouldn't look right for a preacher's daughter to be out on the football field prancing around in such a skimpy skirt." If she agreed not to try out for the squad, he told her, he would buy her a car.

Six months later, Chrissy sneaked out after hours to meet her boyfriend, and was in an accident in that car. When her fuming father came to the police station to get her, Chrissy quickly resorted to her own form of manipulation. "If you punish me, I'll embarrass you in front of the whole town!"

Ignoring

This behavior—running from conflict—is very common to people with a passive-aggressive approach to anger. Parents who use this behavior can go so far as to actually neglect the needs of their children.

An extreme example is a young woman who tearfully stated that she was raped.

"I never knew that!" her mother exclaimed.

"I tried to tell you," the girl cried, "and you just ignored me!"

"You never said he raped you. You just said he wasn't very nice to you."

"That's all I had a chance to say before you changed the subject!" the girl said.

When things are painful, a lot of parents, struggling along in their own denial, will just ignore the whole thing. This is probably the hardest situation to counsel with in family therapy.

Teasing

Teasing is a form of control that makes use of put-downs, humiliation, and sarcasm, all in the name of humor. The secret is *We will hide behind humor instead of telling you what we really think.*

"You computer nerds are all alike," one jock-type man used to tell his computer-loving son. "Guess it doesn't matter that you have no friends. People like you need nothing but your computers."

The family came in for counseling when the boy tried to commit suicide.

Teasing is passed along in families as it is modeled by one generation to the next. The message children get by watching their parents is: This is the way to confront people, to defend yourself, to discipline others, and to handle your anger. Instead of dealing with issues head on, the family learns to tease, always ending with "Just kidding!" or "Can't you take a joke?"

Wise King Solomon wrote: "Death and life are in the power of the tongue" (Prov. 18:21).

Embarrassment

Some people emotionally abuse others by embarrassing them—calling them names, for instance, or acting inappropriately in public, or drinking too much and acting out.

Some parents call their children names in an effort to put the kids in their place. ("Hey, Smarty-pants, pass me the potatoes.") Others do it to direct anger at their children. ("Here comes the jock," a father may say to a bookworm son.)

One boy was called Worms by his family because he could eat anything without gaining a pound. His parents were trying to be funny as a way of building intimacy with the boy, but what they were actually doing was putting up a barrier that would keep all intimacy away. Sadly, they couldn't come out and tell their son, "I love you."

Assigning inappropriate pet names is another way parents try to build closeness with their children without running the risk of really being intimate. One man calls his thirty-year-old married son Hot Rod. It is his way of putting him back into the childish role where he felt closer to his son. But the name angers and embarrasses the young man and drives him farther and farther away from his father.

Repression

People who emotionally abuse by repression refuse to allow other people to acknowledge their feelings. That's how it was in Howard's family. If his son said he was angry, Howard would insist, "Don't be silly, you're not angry. There's nothing to be angry about." If Howard's daughter would start to cry while he was scolding her, he would tell her, "Stop that. You have no reason to cry. If you're going to cry, I'll really give you something to cry about."

It's little wonder that both of Howard's children are now in counseling struggling to learn how to express their emotions.

Verbally Abusive Behaviors

Some people control others by nagging, by condemning, by withering others with sarcasm, or by raging in anger (as discussed in Chapter 4). All of these are forms of verbal abuse. So are some other behaviors that are not quite so obviously abusive, such as controlling another person by exaggerating, by criticizing someone who is meaningful to that person, or by being hypocritical. There is also one behavior that not only is seldom recognized as abusive but also is actually praised as being "Christian." This behavior is strict legalism. No one wants to think of himself as an abuser. The secret underlying verbal abuse is *I can hurt you without feeling guilty because I didn't hit you.*

Nagging

Nagging is a continual condemnation of a person's behavior. People who abuse by nagging are constantly on the backs of those around them—especially their spouses or children. Saying something one time is never enough; it has to be told over and over and over again.

Brenda's grandmother, an obsessive cleaner, was a good example of this kind of nagger. When Brenda cleaned the house, no matter how good a job she did her grandmother always found something that needed fixing. It was never good enough. Although Grandma claimed, "I only wanted Brenda to learn to do it right," the verbal abusiveness was so effective that today Brenda wants nothing to do with her grandmother. She nagged and nagged and nagged until she drove her granddaughter away.

Condemning

Abuse by condemnation doesn't always refer to straight out put-downs. It often takes the form of comparison ("You're just like your irresponsible Aunt Geraldine") or voiced disappointments ("You're a good girl, Pamela, but what I always wanted was a son"). It may even take the form of praise, although the praise is always conditional ("So you're going out for the basketball team. Great! I'll be so proud sitting in the bleachers watching you shooting basket after basket. I always dreamed of having a son who was a star.")

Eddie is an amazingly athletic eleven-year-old. He

is the captain of his youth baseball team, and he even hit a home run in the final all-star game. *Hero* is what his teammates and coach call him. Not his dad. "What's the matter with you?" Eddie's dad yells. "If you had made that last catch, the runner would not have scored!" Poor Eddie. The approval of the coach and other kids on his team is great, but what he really longs for is approval from his dad.

Just this last season the coach has noticed an unfortunate change in Eddie's relationship with his teammates. "All he does is criticize them," he said. Little wonder. Children who live with condemnation learn to condemn. If you have been raised with condemnation, take your motto from Ephesians 4:29: "Let no corrupt word proceed out of your mouth, but what is good for necessary edification, that it may impart grace to the hearers."

Using Sarcasm

Sarcasm—implying that something is true by stating the opposite in a hurtful way—is a deeply painful form of verbal abuse. Sarcasm can be sneering, taunting, or even bitterly cutting.

Bill felt extremely inadequate at work, genuinely afraid that he would be the next one laid off. But he didn't share his fears with his wife. Instead he went home, looked around their cluttered house, and, as his wife came in from her own office job, said, "Oh, my, isn't the house just spotless! You must *really* be tired from all this overwork!"

In counseling, Bill realized that he was dealing with his anger, frustration, and fears by taking them out on his wife. His sarcasm was pushing her away at a time when he needed her the most. But without acknowledging the problem, he replied, "If you want to talk about a smart-mouth, let me tell you about my son. He's as bad as my old man was." Bill's secret is *I feel worthless, so to cover that up, I'll put you down.*

Exaggeration

People who control through exaggeration build themselves up, never being honest about who they really are. Here is how exaggeration was demonstrated in Kyle's, Emma's, and Martin's lives.

Kyle always felt humiliated about having failed algebra and having to take it in summer school in order to graduate. Yet he bragged to his son that he had breezed through math. "I'm not doing your schoolwork for you," he would tell his son when he asked for help. "You're not stupid. You figure it out." Since Kyle, Jr. couldn't figure it out, there was only one conclusion: He really must be stupid. Kyle's exaggeration hurt both him and his son.

A frightened and insecure working mother, Emma constantly exaggerated to her older sister about what a good mother she was. If she baked cookies for one of her children's classes, she would say, "Oh, yes, I'm the room mother this year. I do most of the work myself. I'm never too busy for one of the kids' class parties." Her exaggeration did give her a brief sense of feeling okay about herself, but those positive feelings passed quickly, leaving Emma feeling worse than ever. "Not only am I a crummy mother," she said, "but I'm a liar, too."

Martin felt bad because with the amount of money he earned, his family was bound by a tight budget. To make matters worse, he had just been told that with the economy the way it was, there would be no raises in the foreseeable future. Still, when his wife was fretting over the mounting bills, he told her, "I'll be getting a big raise in the next couple of months." When no raise came through, Martin felt worse than ever. And his wife —who had already spent the promised money—was devastated.

Have you noticed a recurring theme? While exaggeration leads to a short-lived feeling of well-being, it inevitably brings pain to the one who exaggerates as well as to those who are on the other end of the exaggeration. In all these situations, exaggeration hides the secret feeling of low self-esteem.

Playing the Hypocrite

Hypocrites are artificially friendly to those around them. They speak hatefully about others; first behind their backs, then to their faces. Hypocrisy hides its own secret: *I don't like you, but it's not socially correct to let you know that.*

"We are not prejudiced about any people," Mr. Adamson insisted to his daughter, Suzanne. "So why are you always judging our friends?"

"Oh, you're not prejudiced?" Suzanne shot back. "What about the Martins? All you and Mom do is criticize the way they let their kids dress. Then when you see Mr. and Mrs. Martin, you smile sweetly just like everything is great."

The behavior that had shocked the Adamsons in Suzanne was the same two-faced behavior she saw in her parents.

Because most of us are hypocritical at one time or another, Jesus' words in Matthew 7:3 are especially humbling: "And why do you look at the speck in your brother's eye, but do not consider the plank in your own eye?"

Criticizing

Parents can be verbally abusive by pointedly criticizing people who are meaningful to their children. ("Your friend Annie has such bad manners. I just hope they don't rub off on you.") It can also take the form of telling children what to think about people, usually by putting those people down. ("You can't trust anyone who lives in that neighborhood. They are just waiting to take advantage of you.")

Parents insist that their children respect the teacher, then they proceed to cut that teacher down at home. ("What a stupid way to do long division. She obviously knows nothing about teaching math.") Divorced parents tear each other down to the children. ("I can't believe all the crummy things your dad is doing!") People who stress respect for the pastor's message run him down on the way home from church. ("He expects us to willingly come on Sunday, our day off, but no one can get hold of him on *his* day off.") They run down members of their extended family. ("Aunt Susan is so lazy!") This double standard can be extremely confusing to children.

Does this mean that a parent cannot disagree with someone who is important to the child (or a spouse or a relative or a good friend)? Not at all. It simply means that a parent needs to be wise in handling that disagreement. First consider the criticism. Is this a real problem or only a matter of personal opinion? If it's personal opinion, the parent can keep it to herself. If it's a real problem, the parent needs to think of a way to address it without attacking the person.

Operating Under Legalism

The problem with legalism is that it condemns. It leaves no room for differences of opinion or approach. It puts other people down for having different values or lifestyle or goals.

People who operate under legalism are quick to pronounce broad judgment statements upon others. One parent will denounce another parent for the way he raises his child. One Christian will categorically state that another Christian will never make it to heaven because she does things differently or holds a different belief.

It's not unusual for us to hear someone say something such as, "Everyone who goes to parties drinks. So my kids are not allowed to go to any parties at all." If it's a church party? "Well, there might be some wild kids there who will drink, so my kids can't go there, either."

Parents tell their kids such things as:

"You can't go roller-skating because they play secular music at the roller rink."

"You can't spend the night with your friend because her family has a VCR and who knows what you'll be watching."

"You can't go to a birthday party, because Darrel might be there, and he would be a bad influence on you."

Then these parents can't understand why their children are bitter and estranged from them. This is not to say that parents shouldn't have rules. A parent must guide a child but not dictate by more and more rules. Sounds a lot like the Pharisees in Jesus' day, doesn't it? And Jesus certainly never had anything good to say about them.

We can benefit by listening to others whose opinions and ideas differ from our own. By refusing to be caught under rigid legalism, we will free ourselves from a most damaging kind of abuse.

Physical Abuse Secrets

Most people, when they think about abusive behavior, automatically think of physical abuse—children beaten by their parents, wives battered by their husbands, old people terrorized by the younger generation they depend on to care for them.

Although all of these certainly do fall under the category of physical abuse, many less headline-making behaviors are also included. Physically abusive behaviors run the gamut from pushing and shoving, to inappropriate spanking, to actual beatings and torture.

Most people who are guilty of physically abusing the people they are supposed to love are too ashamed to talk about it. That is the terrifying part of this behavior. When it is kept a secret, when it is never faced straight on and handled, it, too, moves right along into the next generation. A young boy watches his father beat his mother, and what registers deep in his mind is, "Well, it must be all right to hit women." Every time a child spills her milk, she is whipped, and when her parents grow old and dependent upon her, guess what? Right! They spill their soup and that old message pops up in her mind that the way to handle such messiness is to strike out.

Physical abuse is actually about power and control. The abusive husband may swear up and down that he loves his wife. The abusing parent may earnestly proclaim his concern for his child. The battering daughter may pledge her devotion to her elderly parents. Yet there is no real intimacy in those relationships. They are control-oriented, all based on "What can you do for me?" And almost all abusive behavior becomes secretive.

The four most common types of physical abuse are

sibling abuse, child abuse, spouse abuse, and abuse of the elderly.

Sibling Abuse

The scenario is surprisingly common: The older sister, the stronger brother, the biggest kid is allowed to control the other siblings by physical force. It happens all the time on television sitcoms. But in real life, for the younger, weaker, smaller brothers and sisters, it is anything but funny. *Why,* they wonder, *can't Mom and Dad feel my pain? Don't they care?*

This is the most common type of physical abuse. Surprised? No wonder. It is also the least talked about. Typically, when the little brother complains to his father about the poundings and jeers he is enduring, Dad says with a shrug, "That's just the way it is when you have a big brother." Parents figure it's no big deal, just brothers and sisters fighting. But sibling abuse is a lot more painful, and far more damaging, than most parents imagine.

Brothers and sisters hurt one another, yet they don't talk about their pain. Parents say, "You guys cut that out," and go back about their business. And then in later years everyone wonders, "Why do you suppose the kids are so distant from one another? They should be friends by now. It really is sad."

Sometimes the generational effects of sibling abuse can be insidious. "When my mother was a girl, she pushed her sister down a ravine and broke her arm," Lorene said. "My mother was really jealous of her because my mother worked hard out in the field and took care of the animals, and her sister stayed in the house and didn't have to do anything. My mother would look at her pampered sister and promise herself in disgust, 'I'll never be like her.'

"Yet when she grew up, my mother's attitude was that the one you love shouldn't have to do anything. She would tell me, 'You don't have to work hard. That's what slave children do.'"

Sometimes parents, with totally good intentions, set their children up to abuse each other. John's brother had a learning disability, and he struggled just to make passing grades. John made all B's and C's in his classes and his parents never said anything about it one way or the other. Their focus was completely on pushing his brother to do better. John was one badge away from Eagle Scout when he quit, basically because no one ever encouraged him to keep on. Yet his parents, in hopes of making things equal, encouraged, pushed, and praised every little thing his brother did. They constantly tried to build up the brother by talking about his accomplishments, but they never mentioned John's for fear of hurting his brother's feelings.

What a perfect set-up for resentment. Today the rivalry is evident in John's family. "My wife is better than your wife," his brother taunts. "My wife cooks and sews and cuts up my food for me. You need to get yourself a real wife." The brother insists it is just a joke, but John sees it differently. "It's the legacy of painful childhood rivalry. It's a battle to prove who is really worthwhile."

Child Abuse

Many people get caught up asking, "Just what is child abuse anyway? Can't I even discipline my kids?"

Some child abuse is so horrible that no one would dispute what it is. But what about kids who are shoved around? Or slapped now and then? Or spanked?

Spanking is an especially volatile subject. How often is it done? How hard? For how long a time? How old is the child? How angry are the parents? Are the parents out of control? Even when these questions are answered, it is difficult to give an accurate definition. Some people say it's okay to spank if you just swat a child twice—but what if that first swat sends him through the wall?

Children who are abused in the name of discipline often believe they deserved what they got. "I was bad," they will say. "It was my fault."

Adults who were raised by physically abusive parents usually take one of two routes: Either they refuse to touch their children at all, or they become physically abusive themselves. Yet even those who never touch their children may be abusive in some other way—such as verbally or emotionally. Because the abuse has taken away their childhood, they either become very serious people who categorically repress anything childlike within themselves, or they become pleasure seekers who don't accept responsibility. By constantly striving to give that child within them a childhood, they refuse to grow up. Most physical abuse is kept secret because of the potential legal problems. An important statistic is that the overwhelming majority (about 80 percent) of abused children do not grow up to be abusive, delinquent, or violent.*

Spouse Abuse

At the lowest level, spousal abuse consists of pushing and shoving and grabbing. Many families who are not necessarily designated as battering engage in this form of abuse. The next level is hitting, then slapping. After that is the terrorizing behavior we typically think of as spouse abuse.

People who are being abused generally respond in one of three ways: They fight back, they try to placate, or they are totally silent. When the abusive episode is over, many couples go into "the honeymoon stage" where the abuser acts rational and calm, even kind and loving. Yet even when the abuser insists he's sorry, he holds on to his conviction that his wife deserved what she got. ("If you weren't so bad, I wouldn't have to throw you around!") And too often, the victim believes it, internalizes it, and thinks, "Yes, I really am bad. If I could just keep my mouth shut this wouldn't happen."

And all the time more and more anger is being generated. It grows and grows, until even the silent

* C. S. Widom, "The Cycle of Violence," *Science*, 244 (1989), 160–165. C. S. Widom, "Does Violence Beget Violence? A critical examination of the literature," *Psychological Bulletin*, 106 (1989), 3–28.

victims struggle to strike back surreptitiously. Women spit in their husbands' food, sabotage their cars and televisions, and even use their husbands' toothbrushes to clean the toilet.

Children who grow up watching one parent abuse the other lose their respect for the victim. "If she has no respect for herself, how can I respect her?" they reason. Then those children grow up to use the same method of control in their own families. Sons, already insecure, see that this is how men get and keep control. What they never see is any pattern of respect for women. The daughters learn from their mothers to play the role of victim.

Richard, raised by a raging father who readily slapped his children, determined to be a different kind of father. While he never hit his children, his own anger showed up in his continual sarcasm and his hair-trigger temper. Richard's son Clifton, now twelve, takes his anger out on his three-year-old sister Jenny. Once while baby-sitting for her, Clifton tied up the little girl and left her crying in her room for over an hour. He mutilates her toys—he once hung her favorite teddy bear from a tree. He continually hits her and threatens her.

"I just can't understand that boy," Richard told us in exasperation.

It is hard enough for Richard to see what both he and his father have done to Clifton. He cannot comprehend the fact that he has actually also abused Jenny, his little darling. Yet already, at the tender age of three,

Jenny is beginning to think, "I must deserve this. This is the way boys treat girls."

Abuse of the Elderly

Elderly people are most often abused by family members who have been charged with their care. A common scenario is an adult who was abused as a child and now has to care for her aged parents in her home. Inevitably, difficulties and disruptions arise, and the child, in turn, becomes abusive of her parents.

"So?" Ralph said when he was accused of beating his elderly father for breaking the coffeemaker. "I learned it from him. Maybe it's just payback time."

When the whole story is known, some people might say Ralph's position is somewhat understandable. However Scripture doesn't agree. In Psalm 71:9 we read: "Do not cast me off in the time of old age; do not forsake me when my strength fails."

Abuse Secrets Move Through the Generations

As in the case of other family secrets, children raised with abuse accept the distorted behaviors as normal. However uncomfortable their situation, children become comfortable with the predictability of the role they have been assigned in their family. ("Lorraine is the beauty, Francine is the one with brains, and Brian is the athlete.") But what happens when Lorraine turns forty-five and she is no longer so beautiful? What about when Francine is out of school and no one cares anymore about her school accomplishments? What will Brian do when the bright lights go off for good and he can no longer play football? Who will they be then?

What happens when the role is destructive from the beginning? ("Poor Fred is the dull one. Maureen is the ugly duckling of the family.") Children thrust into negative roles are destined to grow into adults with low self-esteem, a trait they are likely to carry on to their own children.

Rejecting the Role

"Not me!" Bob told us. "No way! I was always known as the lazy one in my family, but I'm all grown up now, and I refuse to play that part anymore."

He doesn't, either. Today Bob is a full-fledged workaholic who lavishes expensive gifts on his family and enjoys flashing the trappings of his financial success before them. It's his way of saying, "Look what I've got. So who's the lazy one now?"

When people reject their old assigned role, the tendency is to go to the opposite extreme. Adults who were overwhelmed with shows of emotion as children may not allow anyone to express emotions with them when they become adults, not even their spouses or children. They end up emotionally abusing their children by going too far the other way. Children who were ignored tend to smother their own children with overprotectiveness. Those who were teased tend to allow no humor at all in their homes.

The Cost of Keeping the Secret

Here, too, keeping family secrets exacts a high price—the primary cost being physical harm. Another generation is berated and beaten and tormented. The secondary cost may not be as obvious, but it, too, is devastating. Because unresolved bitterness and anger harm the human immune system, those who hold abuse secrets can suffer a whole host of physical problems, such as ulcers, heart attacks, and cancer.

The emotional costs can be crippling as well. Because people who harbor abuse secrets lose the opportunity to have healthy relationships with their own families, they continue the painful dysfunction and pass it along to the next generation. They endure a deep sense of guilt and shame and suffer painfully from low self-esteem. Because they have never learned to establish appropriate emotional boundaries, secret-keepers often have a complete lack of social skills or a lack of common sense. For some the emotional cost is so great that they literally run from their own families. Spiritually, they may run from God, too, in fear or in anger. As one young woman said, "I don't want a heavenly Father! I have a father right here on earth and he's bad enough!"

Healing Hints

If a family has an abuse secret, it looks as if the die is cast. It seems there's nothing anyone can do.

But there is hope. Chapter 11 is all about becoming healthy, but here are a few brief ways to begin to repair the damage of abuse secrets.

1. *Stop the denial and break the silence.* Admit what happened, what it did to you, and how you feel about it.

2. *Set up appropriate physical boundaries.* Refuse to allow others to decide what you should and should not do. Learn to say no. Respect your body.

3. *Develop appropriate emotional boundaries.* Learn to think your own thoughts and make your own decisions. Respect your emotional needs.

4. *Grieve.* Spend as much time as it takes to truly feel all your emotions—the hurt, the anger, the fear. Many people find it helpful to write their experiences and emotions out in a journal—what happened to them, how they felt at the time, how they feel now. If you try this, be sure to express your feelings freely. Cry if you need to. When you have written it out, share your feelings with someone you trust. And talk. Tell your story over and over and over again. Tell it until you no longer need to talk about it. You will not be successful in your journal of healing unless you are willing to walk through your pain.

5. *Experience forgiveness.* Start by forgiving yourself. Refuse to be held captive by false guilt. Then forgive others—the ones who are guilty of the abuse,

and the ones who failed you by not coming to your rescue.

6. *Draw close to God.* Begin by spending time alone with God in prayer. Develop a pattern of reading His word, dwelling on passages that refer to God as your Father and on His love for you. Spend time with others who love God and strive to follow Him.

7

Sexual Secrets

Mark was an unusual man. By almost any standards he was unusual. He tended to overdo everything. A minister, he never tired of telling people that, in his words, "Devout means being willing to be a fool for God." Even this he overdid. Mark's rules and regulations were so strict and rigid that his children became the laughingstock of whatever neighborhood they happened to be living in.

Everyone knew Mark was unusual, but what no one knew was that he was sexually molesting his daughters.

Mark's oldest daughter, Lydia, married at seventeen. What could she know about sexual addictions? All she wanted was to get away from her incestuous father. But within a couple of years she learned a lot, for her own husband was addicted to prostitutes. Lydia read books about handling addictions. She pleaded with her husband to be faithful, cried and yelled and scolded and gave him ultimatums. Finally she persuaded her husband to go with her for counseling. Yet twenty-eight years later, the only difference in Lydia's life is that she lives with the constant fear that her husband will get AIDS and bring it home to her.

Lydia has a tall, handsome, all-American looking son who just turned seventeen. Next week he is going to stand trial on a charge of date rape.

"It's our family," Lydia cried miserably. "There's no hope for any of us."

What a sad situation, all brought about by a family's sexual secrets.

What Causes Sexual Secrets?

Where do such sexual secrets come from? There are a number of causes. One is generational—often the abuser was himself abused as a child. Another is a quest for power and control. The secret-keeper wields a great deal of power in the family and often maintains complete control over everyone else. Another cause is anger. Another is the secret-keeper's own insecurities. Still another is the person's lack of intimacy with those who should be close to him.

Every one of these causes applies to Mark and his family. Generational? Absolutely. Look at his daughter's long-time marriage and the situation with her son. Power and control? Mark ruled his family with an iron fist, and no one dared stand up to him. Anger? You wouldn't have to be with Mark long to see the fury bubbling just beneath the surface. Insecurity? It's obvious in the way he has to constantly brag and praise himself while he condemns and tears down everyone else. Lack of intimacy? Mark has no friends, none of his five children is on speaking terms with him, and his wife says she abides him only because she doesn't believe in divorce. ("He is my cross to bear," she says.)

Forced Sexual Behaviors

Lydia didn't choose the sexual behaviors that were so destructive to her family. They were forced on her. Let's look at the three most common types of forced sexual behaviors—incest, rape, and Satanic Ritual Abuse.

Incest

By definition, incest means sexual intercourse between persons so closely related they are forbidden by law to marry. It is a behavior that is forbidden in almost every culture. And what a destructive secret it is. Incest can easily become the flame that ignites a fire that will burn through the family for generations. Just look at Lydia. Sexually abused by her father, she could not relate to her own husband sexually. That was just the excuse he needed to feed his desire for prostitutes.

Incest is nothing new. It has plagued families since biblical days. Even King David's family was haunted by the terrible consequences after one of David's sons raped his half sister Tamar (see 2 Sam. 13). Today, incest may not lead to civil war, but the consequences still wreak incomprehensible pain and horror on its victims.

Incestuous families share some specific characteristics. Fathers generally are insecure and have poor impulse control. They often grew up witnessing a poor sexual relationship between their own parents, and in fact many were themselves abused as children.

Many times it is a reversal of roles in the family that triggers the incestuous behavior. A man's wife might be disabled, for instance, and his daughter will move in to fill her role in the family. Very often incestuous abusers are restrictive and domineering, and they commonly are jealous parents.

Many of these abusers will point to alcohol or drugs and say, "That's what made me do it! I couldn't help myself, so it isn't my fault." But alcohol and drugs don't *cause* incest, they merely exacerbate the existing problem.

There are mothers who suspect that something is wrong—perhaps that a husband is having an affair, or is losing interest in their marriage, or almost anything but incest. When these mothers find out what is going on they are beyond shock. They are overwhelmed with feelings of anger, revenge, outrage, and guilt for not knowing. But to blame moms for incest is to take the responsibility off the fathers (or grandfathers) where it rightly belongs.

Yet in many cases, mothers in incestuous families are in denial. While some truly don't know what is going on, even they usually have a gut feeling that something isn't right.

When incest is affecting only one child in the family, the other kids may look jealously at that "favorite child" who is getting all the extra attention. When all the children are victimized, it is a different story. Many times the family is made to seem "odd" and encouraged to keep to themselves. Other incestuous families use their ability to socialize to prove their claim that they're healthy. "We all have friends, don't we? And Dad is a deacon in the church."

The scenarios of incestuous families are endless and varied. There are certain categories of children who are more likely to fall prey to incestuous abusers than the average child. The most preyed upon are the mentally ill or delayed. In many cases these children are not able to tell about what is happening to them, or if they do tell, they aren't believed. Next most frequently victimized are the sickly, the weak, and the small. After that are insecure children, those who have a "helpless personality." Children are also more at risk from stepfathers than they are from birth fathers.

Rape

The other form forced sexual behavior commonly takes is rape, a devastatingly destructive secret with plenty of guilt dished out to the victim. Why?

One reason is that it isn't talked about. Another reason is shame and embarrassment. Another is fear—the attacker may have made threats. And underlying the tragedy is the thought that lingers in so many people's minds: She must have been doing *something* wrong. So the victim, and many times her family as well, tries to hide what happened.

While families usually make an effort to be supportive, hurtful messages do come through.

- "Are you sure you didn't ask for it?"
- "You shouldn't have been there in the first place."
- "Your clothes encouraged it."
- "Why didn't you fight?"
- "What did you do to bring it on?"
- "It's your punishment for being rebellious."
- "Of course it's not your fault, but you did . . ."

Satanic Ritual Abuse

This movement is a frightening—and growing—source of sexual family secrets. Satanic Ritual Abuse (SRA) is just what the name implies—Satan worship that involves ritualistic sexual abuse, often among family members. In some areas of the country it is becoming frighteningly prevalent. Some of these abusers are even church members; church involvement makes a good disguise.

The activities in which these practitioners participate can be truly horrific. Certain family members are actually raised for the sole purpose of being "breeders"; that is, to have babies who can be used as sacrifices. One woman related that at one such gathering, her father had passed her around to the people in attendance. We have talked to several people who told of being cut, brainwashed, and burned and even having drunk the blood of sacrifice victims.

At a conference of the Consortium of California Child Abuse Councils in 1987, Dee Brown, a journalist who has been a leader since 1984 of reporting the "almost unbelievable" experiences of SRA survivors, gave a presentation on SRA. Based on her interviews with adult survivors, she stated, "Six out of six reported consumption of feces, blood and urine, and drugs. Four out of six said the perpetrators wore robes. Five out of six said that the perpetrators were important people, i.e., doctors, dentists, religious figures . . . who were basically the solid backbone of the community. Five out of six discussed incest as being part of their family environment. Four out of six described that these experiences happened under the guise of a traditional, fundamentalist Christian group. . . . The same people who were involved on a daily basis in the Christian aspects of religious worship were involved in the satanic aspects at night."[1]

The entire movement, which is now occurring nationwide, is tied in with sexual abuse. There are two kinds of SRA. *Intrafamilial SRA* occurs within the family, usually as part of a pattern that goes on for generations. Victims are raised in cult families and locked into its secrets from the beginning of their lives.

[1]Friesen, James G. 1991. *Uncovering the Mysteries of MPD.* San Bernardino, Calif.: Here's Life Publishers.

Extrafamilial SRA most often occurs in day care settings, where the tiny victims are ritualized as two-, three-, and four-year-olds.

Either way, most often SRA is not discovered. Perpetrators are often very intelligent, imaginative people who do not want to be caught, so they carefully hone their cover-up skills. The damage suffered by victims is immense, for a few perpetrators can spread fear and destruction among many families. According to the video *America's Best Kept Secret*, "From the number of preschool cases alone, it would appear that a massive indoctrination of American children into Satanism is going on." Yet the public hears relatively little about it.

Chosen Sexual Behavior

Such victimizations as incest, rape, and SRA are indeed tragic. Yet not all sexual secrets are forced upon people. Sometimes the behaviors are chosen.

Chosen sexual behavior includes extramarital affairs, pornography, and involvement with multiple sex partners.

Extramarital Affairs

If the statistics are to be believed, fully half the population engages in at least one affair sometime during their marriage. Most shocking is the frequency with which sexual infidelity occurs within the Christian community.

Earlene and Harold were having so many problems

that Earlene confided to her friends that she wished she could just get out of the marriage and start over again. In the months that followed, Earlene found constant reasons for Karla, an attractive widow they knew from the neighborhood, to be around the house. "She's lonely," Earlene would explain. "She needs to be with people." When Karla had trouble with her car, Earlene quickly suggested, "Harold will come over and look at it. He is so handy with cars." Soon it was, "If you need a ride, Karla, Harold will take you," and "Harold would be happy to spend a few hours Saturday morning fixing up your yard—especially if you reward him with a lemon meringue pie. It's his favorite."

To Harold, Earlene would say, "Karla feels so comfortable around you. It's really nice that she has you to confide in." When the morning yard touch-ups stretched into the afternoon, then until dinnertime, Earlene said to her husband, "I understand. Karla needs someone to be there for her."

Before long, Harold and Karla became involved in an affair. Earlene immediately said, "Well, it's obvious that our marriage problems are not my fault! Harold is just a lowlife. Biblically I can get a divorce now." Earlene had set Harold up for an affair.

Again and again people ask, Why are affairs so much more common in the church than in business? It may just seem that way, but certainly there are factors to consider. At church, everyone is friendly, everyone is trusting, everyone feels safe. Because the people at church are coming from the same spiritual foundation, an intimate bond develops among them. People don't have their guard up as they do in a secular workplace.

When a particular woman was going through tough times, her pastor went to her home night after night to pray her through her troubles. If this had been a boss and a secretary, the husband would have had a fit. But since it was a minister and his parishioner, the husband figured it was all right.

In many cases, men in positions of power begin to see sexual conquests as within their rightful domain. That's why there are so many instances of extramarital affairs among politicians, high-profile pastors, high-powered attorneys, and doctors. The scenario is typical: The man is a partner in a prestigious law firm. Everyone in his office—the secretaries, law clerks, and paralegals —tells him how wonderful he is, what great work he does, how compassionate he is, or what a good listener he is. Then he goes home to his wife who is angry because he didn't take out the trash and kids who are far more interested in talking on the telephone to their friends than in talking to him about his accomplishments of the day. Since he has so little time and attention left for his family anyway, they certainly don't feel like showering him with praise.

The stage is set. Before long, this man may well be drawn into an affair with someone who shows him the respect he is convinced is due him. Or it may be that his wife will get involved with someone who thinks she is important enough to warrant some priority.

Other times affairs simply reflect a lack of respect

for women. In our society, there is often a double standard. Those who have seen no evidence of consequences in society or in their own families from extramarital affairs may well assume that there *are* no consequences. If a parent never confronts the erring spouse but stays passively by his side, the child will learn it must be okay.

Yet regardless of the pressures people have on them or how much they rationalize, God's commandment is clear: "You shall not commit adultery" (Ex. 20:14).

Pornography

Pornography has reached astonishing proportions in today's society, both in availability and in public acceptance. More and more people are saying, "So what if I enjoy pornography? It's not hurting anyone. It's my business what I read and watch and listen to, and no one else's."

But pornography is indeed hurting someone else: the ones who participate in it, those who are exploited to prepare it, the families of those who look at it, and, yes, even society at large. How?

Contrary to what many people believe, pornography is addictive. Like drugs, it actually causes an addictive high.

Since most users of pornography are men and most pornographic subjects are women (or children!), it fosters a most demeaning and destructive attitude toward women, who are depicted as slaves, victims, or mere sex objects.

"Maybe some people are affected that way, but not me," Jeffrey insisted. "I get my wife to watch erotic videos with me, and we use them as an aid to our marriage and sexual relationship. So for us it's a good thing."

Jeffrey wasn't getting a "marriage aid" at all. What he was getting was a false sense of intimacy with his wife. That wasn't her up there on the screen. The words spoken weren't spoken to each other. No real intimacy comes from a movie or a magazine or a voice on the telephone.

Jeffrey told us that his father had always had a stack of erotic magazines discreetly stacked under his bed. "Dad wasn't doing anything wrong, and he certainly wasn't hurting anyone," Jeffrey insisted. "No one even knew."

Jeffrey knew. He had been sneaking into his parents' bedroom to "read" for years. Once when his father caught him, his dad simply laughed and walked out. What Jeffrey got from his father was passive permission to "enjoy a little cheesecake." Now, years later, Jeffrey has long since progressed from a reader of his dad's naughty but acceptable magazines. Today he is deeply addicted to hard-core pornography.

Clifford was different. He was always taught that sex was nasty and bad. He loves and respects his wife, but because of his early lessons, he has a poor sexual relationship with her. He has turned to pornography as a poor substitute for the intimacy and sexual closeness he should be finding at home.

It's not always fathers who pass a tendency toward pornography on to their children. Mothers who suffer from low self-esteem can pass along the idea that women are not all that worthwhile, certainly not as worthy as men. Without ever putting it into words, the message comes through loud and clear.

Scripture has some very definite instructions about what we are to put into our minds. In Philippians 4:8 we read: "Finally, brethren, whatever things are true, whatever things are noble, whatever things are just, whatever things are pure, whatever things are lovely, whatever things are of good report, if there is any virtue and if there is anything praiseworthy—meditate on these things."

Multiple Sexual Partners

Unlike pornography, multiple sexual partners is not an addiction seen mainly in men. Women, too, are trapped in this behavior. A number of family situations can cause a need for multiple sexual partners. It may be that as a child the person never got the love she needed, either because her own parents were withdrawn or cold and distant or absent. So now as an adult she continues to seek that love—only she equates sex with love.

A girl may have been raised hearing that she was a tramp or a slut. So when she grows up, sure enough, she manages to live down to the expectations.

For men, it's different. Often a boy has grown up being told, "If you're going to be a real man, you have to have sex. The more women you have, the more of a man you are." One father went so far as to seek out prostitutes for his son when he was a teenager so that they could initiate him into manhood. Other fathers brag to their sons about their own sexual prowess and conquests.

Sex does *not* equal love. This is an easy myth to buy into, for it is proclaimed everywhere—in the movies, on television, in books. When people hear it at home as well, the myth becomes a deeply ingrained part of their belief system. Conversely, for some people, having many sexual partners feels safer than having to be close and loving to just one person. It protects them from having to get too intimately involved.

Irresponsible sexual behavior, often carried out in secret, may result in out-of-wedlock pregnancies. Such pregnancies can then lead to further secret-keeping, abortions, or forced marriages.

Results of Sexual Behavior

Out-of-Wedlock Pregnancy

"I had a baby when I was fifteen years old," Dena said. "The baby was put up for adoption before I saw it. I don't even know if it was a girl or a boy. That's how I wanted it, because I decided I would just go on with my life as if the whole horrible pregnancy had never happened."

It didn't work. Denial never does. For the past five years Dena has been agonizing over the loss of the child she never knew. Only now is she beginning to move through the grieving process.

A woman named Sherry said, "Even though I wasn't married, I was excited when I found out I was pregnant. I would finally have someone who would really love me."

Motherhood turned out to be more difficult than Sherry had ever dreamed. Her idealistic imaginings turned out to be nothing but false security.

When a birth becomes a family secret and no one talks about it, no one explains how to prevent it from happening again. No one talks about the pain it caused, either. And no one says that although it was a mistake, it need not be a scarlet letter to be worn forever.

"My parents did everything they could to hide what had happened from everyone—even their closest friends and our relatives," said Dena. "They would tell me, 'We really love you,' but I sure didn't feel loved."

"My mother was okay with my baby," Sherry said, "but my dad was furious. He had always told me, 'I don't care what you do with your life, just don't go and get yourself pregnant.' My mom told me, 'I accept you for who you are, but let's not tell your dad. There is no telling what he might do.' When Dad found out, he was so mad at my mom for standing up for me. In the end, it broke up their marriage."

Abortion

"I knew I had done a horrible thing by having sex with my boyfriend," Claire told us. "Then when I got pregnant, I knew everyone else would know it, too. Everyone would talk about me as the bad girl. They'd call me a slut and a tramp. I couldn't stand that."

So rather than carry the child to term and publicly expose her shame, Claire decided to have an abortion. She continued to carry her shame, only now it was tucked down deep within her soul.

Claire's family had always had high expectations of their attractive, talented daughter. "They wanted me to be the best at everything," Claire said. "I couldn't be just a cheerleader—I had to be head cheerleader. I couldn't just get good grades—I had to get all A's, and they had to be in the advanced placement classes. I couldn't just date—I had to date *great* guys. I did all that. So how could I let my parents down by having an illegitimate baby?"

Eilene's reason for getting an abortion was different. "I just couldn't have a baby," she said. "I would lose a semester in college and I wouldn't graduate with my class." Eilene's reason is common—pregnancy and childbirth are just too inconvenient. Furthermore, she had never learned to delay gratification. She worked this problem out just as she worked out most other inconveniences in her life: She was uncomfortable, so she wanted the matter fixed *now*.

Behavior has its consequences. Perhaps this truth is

never so apparent as in an unwanted pregnancy. Many women who have abortions—and often their parents as well—will say, "I don't believe in abortion as a rule, but this situation is different." The most common reason that women seek abortions is that they are unable to accept the responsibility of their pregnancy.

Abortion can be a tremendously painful secret to keep. Women have abortions for many reasons, and many, if not most, suffer because of them. We can know what God thinks about life from Psalm 139:13–16:

> For You formed my inward parts;
> You covered me in my mother's womb.
> I will praise You, for I am
>   fearfully and wonderfully made;
> Marvelous are Your works,
> And that my soul knows very well.
> My frame was not hidden from You,
> When I was made in secret,
> And skillfully wrought in the
>   lowest parts of the earth.
> Your eyes saw my substance
>   being yet unformed.

But we also know that God loves us and forgives us. In 1 John 1:9 we read: "If we confess our sins, He is faithful and just to forgive us our sins and to cleanse us from all unrighteousness."

Forced Marriage

Of course there is an option to an unwanted pregnancy other than having an out-of-wedlock child or getting an abortion. The woman can get married. It used to happen far more often than it does today. In the past most couples would say, "People mustn't know what we have done, so we'll hide it by quickly getting married."

Nor is marriage always the young person's idea. The message may come from the parents: "If you don't get married, it will make the whole family look bad. You have got a responsibility to us."

And when the baby comes, certainly no one wants to let him or her in on the nasty secret. No one wants to tell the child that her parents got married because her mother was pregnant.

The Simon family came in for counseling because their older son, twelve-year-old Nicholas, was causing trouble at school. "He has always been a problem," Mrs. Simon said before they had even settled in their seats. It didn't take long to see that both parents kept this child at arm's length. Later, when Nicholas was out of the room, his parents admitted that they had gotten married because he was on the way. "He's not the same as his brother and sister," Mr. Simon said. "They were planned. But Nicholas, well, if he hadn't come along I could have finished college and I'd have a decent job today." These parents had blamed their baby for the untimeliness of his birth, and now, twelve years later, they were still ashamed of him.

To his parents' utter astonishment, Nicholas already knew he had caused his parents' marriage, and he had carried the shame and guilt within him his entire life.

The Cost of Sexual Secrets

Families that harbor sexual secrets suffer greatly. Because they never feel comfortable with their own sexual identity, they are unable to be intimate with each other. Instead of husband and wife experiencing sexual contentment through true intimacy, they seek sexual highs vicariously, as through pornography. Many men and women who have never dealt with their own sexual abuse participate in sex merely out of a sense of duty. They are never able to fulfill their own lives in this area. And because they are not comfortable with sex, they do all they can to stay away from it.

Little wonder the couple becomes more and more distanced from each other, until they begin to lose the relationship altogether. The result is a depth of pain that is almost unbearable. One or both become involved in an affair, or perhaps one or the other takes solace in drugs or alcohol.

In time, this pulling away can even cost parents their relationships with their children. Perhaps one of the saddest things of all is that once sexual abuse has occurred within the family, it's very difficult for the family to go back. Unless they all work toward God's restoration, their relationship is forever affected.

Sexual abuse is one of the most hurtful and damaging things one person can do to another. Not only does it break the body, but it also breaks a person's soul.

Children who never learn to set appropriate boundaries never learn to respect themselves. Nor do they ever learn to respect others. Either they set no boundaries at all or they erect around themselves what one counselor calls "The Great Wall of China." They say in effect, "No human will ever hurt me again."

Families that harbor sexual secrets never experience the fullness of sex as God intended it. Because the secret causes the family members to lose their sense of integrity, it is terribly damaging to their self-esteem. They look at people and think, "I know what you see when you look at me, but that's not what I really am."

Because they have not sought forgiveness for themselves, those who harbor the secrets have a great deal of trouble accepting the forgiveness of God. Even the abusers say, "I'm so bad, I'll probably be this way the rest of my life." This is an especially difficult hurdle, for it almost gives them an excuse to keep on doing what they have been doing.

But God can forgive, and He can change lives. And that begins with accepting the responsibility for your actions and to ask God for His forgiveness.

This is the only way to break the power of sexual secrets.

Healing Hints

Even those who have suffered sexual abuse can stop carrying the secret. The following steps can help you break free.

1. Start by admitting to yourself the truth of what happened.

2. Tell someone you can trust, someone who will listen to you as you tell your story and will pray for your healing.

3. Seek professional help to share your secret and gain therapeutic insight.

4. Accept the significance of the story of Jesus Christ and accept His healing and grace as a role model for your life.

5. With the help of a professional, decide when, how, or whether to confront the abuser.

6. Set up appropriate boundaries for yourself in relationships.

7. Give yourself time to heal.

8. Grieve the loss by writing, talking, crying, and praying over and over. This will help you express the entire range of your feelings.

9. Forgive yourself and turn the abuser over to God for Him to deal with after your time of grieving.

10. Talk about the secret to trusting family and friends.

11. Break the secret by role modeling healthy behaviors in relationships.

12. Break the secret by helping your children to be educated sexually and to know how to protect themselves from sexual abuse.

13. Join a support group to help you understand the dynamics of your sexual secret.

For those who are abusers, or who are still keeping the secret of past abusive behavior, the following steps can help them break free of the behavior and the secret.

1. Accept the power of healing through Jesus Christ.

2. Admit you have a sexual problem. To help you break the denial and start facing your problems, write down the exact nature of your problem.

3. Seek professional help to gain therapeutic insight into your problem.

4. Get an accountability partner of the same sex with whom you can talk openly about your feelings and thoughts.

5. Join a support group to help you understand the dynamics of your behavior.

6. Don't blame the victim or others for your actions. Accept full responsibility for your behavior.

7. Ask forgiveness from God for your behavior. Ask forgiveness from the victim and from other family members who have been hurt by your actions. (Give them time to work through their own grief. They may not be ready—or able—to forgive you right now, or to accept your forgiveness. This is not your responsibility. You are only responsible for your actions.)

8. Explore your behaviors and thoughts which have lead to your sexual secrets, and find appropriate ways to deal with those feelings, thoughts, or insecurities.

9. Renew your mind daily. This means starting to face your thoughts and feelings by exploring why they are there. Then begin to replace the lies with the truth that Christ provides.

One final warning: Some sexual secrets must by law be reported to the appropriate authorities. For a perpetrator, coming forward with a willingness to work on the problem will only help. Even though there may still be consequences for the behavior, half the battle will have been won by voluntarily stepping forward.

8

Secrets of Circumstance

The Andreas family was nice enough, although, as the neighbors said, "They kept to themselves." Still, when Mrs. Andreas went out to check the mail or Mr. Andreas mowed the lawn, they would always greet their neighbors with a friendly wave and a smile. The Andreas children didn't play much with the other kids in the neighborhood, but they were well behaved and certainly never caused any trouble.

Martin, their twelve-year-old son, could have told a different story. Martin was repeatedly grounded because of his bad grades at school. His angry father frequently yelled, "Why are you so stupid? Why can't you understand what the teacher explains like the other kids do?" Other times he threatened, "You will never watch TV or play with your friends again if you don't quit being so lazy and do some studying!"

Martin did feel different. It was so hard to concentrate with all the noise at school and so hard to sit still. He was ashamed that he had disappointed his father.

Because the Andreas family could not discuss their

"secret," they couldn't get the help they needed. Martin was neither stupid nor lazy. He suffered from attention deficit disorder, a problem that could have been helped with counseling and medication.

In some families, family secrets don't start with a problem of victimizing anyone. They come from the *circumstances* of their lives. Members of their families suffer from mental problems, learning disabilities, deformities, or handicaps. The circumstance may even be something as seemingly innocuous as having been raised in a poor family.

The Secrets of Circumstance

Any difficult situation a family is called upon to deal with secretively becomes a secret. But some circumstances are especially prone to grow into circumstantial family secrets.

Mental Illnesses

This is probably the category into which the highest number of circumstantial family secrets fall. There is something frightening about the incomprehensible workings of an ill mind; there is something unreachable in mental illness, and many family members are extremely uncomfortable.

Duncan's brother, Neil, suffered from schizophrenia. "My parents just couldn't handle Neil's problem," Duncan said. "All they could think of was my father's brother, Uncle Theo, who everyone whispered about being *strange.*" Because they were unable to face the fact that Neil might be suffering from the same affliction that haunted Uncle Theo, they didn't get their son the treatment he needed. "The truth is," Duncan said, "my mother and father were too ashamed of my brother to get him help." Even worse, the family never talked about it. Everyone acted as though there was nothing wrong with him. It was as if the other family members thought if they ignored the problem, it would go away.

Duncan sought counseling because he needed to know what to tell his own son.

"I've tried to pretend to him that nothing is wrong with Neil, but he's asking more and more questions," he said. "How can I get my little boy to see Neil as just a normal uncle?"

The family secret was moving on to the next generation.

Alice's children stopped having friends over to the house because their mother was depressed. They never knew what the place would look like, or even if their mother had gotten out of bed that day. They also began to wonder if they might be to blame for their mother's depression. "I think it's my fault," Alice's thirteen-year-old daughter said in tears. "I should be a better kid."

Schizophrenia and clinical depression are two mental conditions that can easily develop into family secrets. Another is breaking from reality, a condition called a "psychotic break."

Nathan was a wonderful husband and father. Although he worked in a demanding job ten hours a day, six days a week, he never failed to make time to coach his son's soccer team and his daughter's softball team, and to lead a Boy Scout troop. When the church choir director left, he volunteered to fill in, a temporary position that had lasted almost two years. Everyone who knew Nathan pointed to him and said, "Now *there's* a wonderful man. His family is so lucky!"

One evening, long after the family had gone to bed, Nathan's wife heard a strange sound coming from the family room downstairs. When she went to see what was going on, she found Nathan standing naked in the middle of the room crying his eyes out. She couldn't talk to him, she couldn't comfort him, she couldn't reason with him, she couldn't get him to put his clothes on. In desperation she called an ambulance, and Nathan was taken to a mental hospital.

All three—Neil, Alice, and Nathan—finally each got help. Yet without treatment, they would likely have stayed in their ill state for a long period of time, and would most likely have gotten worse. That's why a mental health family secret is triply destructive: It harms the family, it harms the sufferer, and, as we have seen so often before, it harms the generations to come.

A related area of family secrets, but one that does not really fall under the heading of mental illness, is that of eccentricity. An eccentric person can be defined as someone who deviates from accepted conduct. An eccentric's appearance and behavior are exaggerated, and many members of the eccentric's family would describe him as "embarrassing."

One such woman is about sixty. She wears either a pink or purple miniskirt and a matching ruffled blouse, piles of necklaces and bracelets, and huge dangling earrings. Her hair, dyed bright red, is sprayed into big curls and elaborate wings. She calls everyone "Honey" and "Sweetie," and she is not what most of us would picture as an ideal grandmother.

We live in a society that rewards conformity. It's okay to be a little different, but not *too* different. And when we see that someone in our family is sticking out and acting inappropriately, the temptation is to turn our backs on that person. But that is not the way Jesus sees it. In Matthew 25:40, after He has talked of caring for people who are in need of help—hungry, thirsty, strangers, naked, sick, in prison—we read: "And the King will answer and say to them, 'Assuredly, I say to you, inasmuch as you did it to one of the least of these My brethren, you did it to Me.' "

Mental Retardation

All prospective parents anticipate a wonderful baby, the best baby ever. They see themselves as the parents of darling children, all bright and alert, all healthy and sound. When that perfect baby turns out to be mentally retarded, the shattered dreams, the pangs of guilt, all the unanswered questions, all the nagging what-ifs, can turn into shame and denial.

But mental retardation is, in itself, not a dysfunction. It only becomes a dysfunction when it is dealt with in secrecy and shame.

Learning Disabilities

Learning disabilities make especially ironic secrets, for when they are recognized, they may well be treatable, even correctable. Even so, there are many children whose problems are multiplied by their families' shame and embarrassment.

The Carsons were an intellectual family. Dr. Carson was a physicist; his wife a computer programmer. They had two bright children who were always at the top of their classes throughout their school years. Then along came Carrie. As a child, she struggled and struggled, yet she was never able to make it out of the bottom of her class.

No one in the Carson family ever acknowledged Carrie's problems. When her parents were called in for conferences with her teachers, they would say, "Carrie is just inclined to be lazy. We will get onto her about her work and she will do better."

Even when extensive testing showed that Carrie's problem was dyslexia, the Carsons refused to accept it, and the tests were never mentioned again. The reason Carrie's problem was never talked about was that it was understood in the Carson family that Carsons did not have children who were "slow." Therefore, Carrie *couldn't* have trouble learning. And so, year after year, Carrie was pushed to succeed, even though she could not.

The Carsons were a dysfunctional family, but it wasn't because of Carrie's dyslexia. It was because her family refused to support her special needs. It was because they could not accept their daughter for who she was.

Deformities and Handicaps

It's amazing the abnormalities that can deeply distress a family. Even something as minor as crossed eyes can become a family secret. Some families with children who suffer handicaps are so embarrassed by their children's conditions that they won't take them anywhere. Then it becomes an isolation issue.

Penny has a brother who was born severely handicapped. "I am ashamed to admit it, but I grew up burning with anger at the attention my brother got," Penny says. "To make matters worse, I wasn't able to do so many of the things I wanted to do, because we never could afford the cost. Everything we had went for him."

Today Penny is the mother of two healthy boys. "I can tell you one thing, my children are being raised a lot differently than I was," she boasts. "Neither of my boys has ever been treated better than the other one. Yet they are angry at me. They both insist I'm unfair. I can't understand what they are talking about."

The boys have their own side of the story to tell. "I have to play football, and I hate it!" Clay says. "I'm terrible at it. I spend every game sitting on the bench. But since Jeremy likes football, I have to play, too."

"Big deal!" says Jeremy. "How do you think I feel taking stupid music lessons? Just because you want to play drums, I have to waste all my free time practicing on that old trumpet."

Penny is so obsessed with her determination to treat her sons exactly alike that she doesn't take their individual needs into consideration. All because of her family secret.

Poverty

When Joel was a teenager, he was embarrassed by his family. "We were poor," he said. "We lived in a crummy neighborhood. We drove crummy cars. I never had decent clothes like everyone else had. Whenever I asked for something, even if it was really important to me, my parents would say, 'Sorry, Joel, we can't afford it.' Well, that's not what I say to my children. My kids have all those things I never had because we *can* afford it!"

Of course, Joel isn't able to spend very much time with his children, because he is too busy making that money to spend on them.

If anyone were to suggest to Joel that he is perpetuating the problem of his own family, he would vigorously protest. But that is exactly what he is doing. He is passing along to his children the very same message he learned in his own youth: "Never mind true intimacy. You show your love by the things you give."

A family doesn't have to actually be poor for the members to harbor a secret of poverty. One little boy who lived in a nice neighborhood wished with all his heart he could live in his friend's huge elaborate house. He was so embarrassed by his "poverty" that he wouldn't invite any other kids to his own perfectly fine home.

Regardless of whether the poverty is real or perceived, the secrets that result from it can be painful and controlling.

Reasons for Perpetuating the Secret

Many families have situations that they wish they could change, but not all circumstances develop into full-blown secrets. Circumstantial secrets are perpetuated because of the family messages they pass along. These are often faulty assumptions the family holds that cause them not to tell. Here are some of the most destructive of these messages.

MESSAGE 1: "We don't want to know."

This is the message that insists, "Ignorance is bliss." Some families never do come to where they can really comprehend a challenging circumstance. This is especially true of mental illness. The stigma is just too strong. If the family doesn't know, if they are not able to understand, then they won't have to deal with it.

MESSAGE 2: "We are different and ashamed."

This is a message of fear. People shy away from a family member with some particular problem. The family feels obligated to justify that person or to back that person up. "Our daughter has Down's syndrome," one young mother said. "I'm so sick of explaining her situation to strangers."

But when asked if strangers asked questions— "Well, no," the young woman admitted. "But I know they are looking at her and wondering."

MESSAGE 3: "If we don't tell, no one will know."

This is a message of embarrassment. If people know that a family member is "different," there may be a lot of unwanted questions asked. So isn't it better to just keep the whole thing quiet? As the immediate problem eases, the family message develops and the family conspires to lock the secret away.

MESSAGE 4: "If we pretend there is no problem, then there isn't a problem."

Many families simply refuse to acknowledge that there is any problem at all. This is an especially damaging message, because if no one admits there is a problem, then no one gets any help. And if no one gets any help, the secret goes on and on.

MESSAGE 5: "What other people think of us is more important than the truth."

This is a message that instructs the family to keep up appearances regardless of the cost. If a family member is different from so-called normal people, others might react negatively. And most of us have been raised to avoid the stigma of society.

The Cost of Keeping the Secret

As detailed again and again in the previous chapters, keeping a secret comes with an incredibly high price tag. Here are some of the costs of harboring circumstantial secrets:

It Breaks Up Family Intimacy

When a family cannot accept all of its members, people isolate themselves from one another or overcompensate with overprotection. In either case, there can be no intimacy where there are no appropriate boundaries. Not only do isolated family members withhold the support others in the family need, but they send a powerful message to their children. "Being different," they teach, "is not acceptable."

It Creates Reaction Formation

Reaction formation means going to the opposite extreme. Kimberly is an example of this. Her mother, at two hundred fifty pounds, is definitely obese. Kimberly is so obsessed with being thin that she recently was hospitalized with anorexia. At five feet five inches, Kimberly weighs just eighty-nine pounds.

The oldest child in the Tomasi family is mentally retarded. The rest of the family is preoccupied with learning and becoming educated, as if to prove, "I am not retarded! I am okay!"

It Develops Prejudice

Anyone, confronted with the challenge of seeing dysfunctional relatives and dealing with their problems, runs the risk of becoming judgmental toward them. "Why don't you just lose weight?" we may demand in exasperation. Or "Snap out of your depression." Responding to family members with a lack of understanding can easily lead to a condemning attitude toward *all* people who are different.

It Prevents Us from Finding the Potential

Refusing to accept people the way they are blocks the appreciation of the special abilities God has given to different individuals. Although God doesn't make every person beautiful and intelligent, He does make each person precious and worthwhile.

It Encourages Overcriticism

Criticizing challenged family members increases the risk of becoming overly critical about everything and everyone who does not appear to be perfect.

It Leads to Rejection

Imagine the pain of being denied by your own family. To refuse to accept people as they are is in effect to deny that they exist. This denial of a family member feeds upon itself, for it requires a great deal of secrecy. The result is a complete break of trust from one generation to the next.

It Bars Enjoyment

One terrible cost of keeping the secret is that members of the family never get to truly enjoy intimacy with other members in their family. When we don't confront our feelings about a family member who happens to be different, when we consistently push that person away, when we isolate ourselves from members of our family who refuse to keep the secret, we erect a system of anger and distrust. It is this anger and distrust that sabotages all the relationships in the family.

How very costly the secret-keeping is. And how very sad.

Moving Toward Healing

Every family *can* make changes, no matter how long the secrets have been kept. Every family can move toward healing. Here are some healing hints that will help your family along:

1. *Be willing to accept all family members as they are.* Whether actually dysfunctional or just struggling with some challenging situation, every person in the family deserves to be accepted.

2. *Find value in all people.* Don't limit sights to those in the family. Look for the strengths and the abilities and the worth in every person.

3. *Learn to enjoy the differences among people.* It is easy to look askance at anyone who is "different." Differences make us uncomfortable. Step back and learn to appreciate and enjoy the many ways that individuals are unique.

4. *Become knowledgeable about the disability.* What are the issues involving the family member's specific condition? What are his limitations? What are her potentials? What can be changed and what must just be accepted? Get information, contact support networks, keep up on the latest developments and treatments.

5. *Be able and willing to express yourself.* Hurts? Feelings of guilt? Shame? Talk about your feelings. Hiding or denying them will only deepen the secret and give it more power.

6. *Encourage the family member to get help.* Some people need little more than encouragement, and they will willingly accept help. Others need great amounts of prodding and support before they will agree. Be ready to offer your family member the help and encouragement he or she needs. If the family member will not cooperate no matter what, then learn to live with the situation. You cannot make another person do what he or she refuses to

do. Part of your own personal healing includes letting go in love.

7. *Don't keep the secret.* At first, telling the secret may cause shame and discomfort—but it will also bring relief. In return for breaking the silence, you will receive the understanding and support you so desperately need in order to begin your own healing process.

8. *Pray for the family member.* Bring the situation before the Lord and trust Him to work with the family member. Ask God to give you the strength and wisdom to handle the situation in the best way possible. As you turn the matter over to Him, let go of the responsibility for changing the other person's condition. Sometimes, when you are struggling with a difficult circumstance, you may come to the place where it seems too hard to go on. God has provided many comforting promises for you in His Word. One such promise is, "For He has not despised nor abhorred the affliction of the afflicted; nor has He hidden His face from Him; but when He cried to Him, He heard" (Ps. 22:24).

9

Adoption Secrets

Adoption. Isn't this all about putting family-less little ones into homes with people whose greatest desire is to be parents? What a wonderful, positive situation. How can there be harmful family secrets here?

Consider the tales of three adoptions.

Claudia's Story

Claudia was only three days old when she was adopted through a state adoption agency. She will never forget the day she learned how she had made her entrance into her family.

"It was a warm spring day when I was in second grade," Claudia said. "On the way home from school, I got into a tussle with my friend Elizabeth, whose mother was my mother's best friend. 'You don't know anything!' I told Elizabeth.

" 'I know more than you do!' she shot back. 'I know that you were adopted!'

"I ran home in tears to ask my mother if Elizabeth's words were true. After hemming and hawing around in a very nervous way, my mother finally said, yes, I was adopted. She said she and Daddy always planned to tell me about it, but that they just never found the right time and the right words. I knew right away that adoption had to be something bad. Friends don't blurt out good things when they are angry with you. And mothers don't hem and haw and act nervous when they have good news to tell. And it doesn't take mothers and fathers years to find the right time and the right words to tell you something good.

"As I grew up, I became more and more curious about me before the adoption. Who was I? Why had I been given up? Who were those other parents who gave me life? My mother and father claimed they knew nothing about my beginnings, and they acted so uncomfortable when I asked questions that I finally gave up my quest.

"My entire adoption is one big secret that no one talks about unless forced to. So is my background. I don't even know my national heritage. And heaven forbid I should ever need to know anything about my medical history! It's as if I just popped out of the ground at the age of three days and fell into the family I call my own."

Maria's Story

"I was sixteen when I got the surprise of my life," Maria said. "The whole family was at our house for Christmas, and I overheard my aunts talking. My Aunt

Juanita said, 'I think Maria should know that Maxine is her grandmother and not her mother.' As it turns out, the woman I had always called Mama was actually my grandmother, the man I called Daddy was my grandfather, and the truck driver aunt who lived across the country was my mother."

Maria never was actually given up for adoption. When she was born, her fifteen-year-old unmarried mother brought her baby home to live. But within a few years, Maria's mother grew tired of being tied down by motherhood. More and more she resumed her teenage life, turning the care of her daughter over to her own mother and father. By the time Maria started kindergarten, the family had "just happened."

"Everybody knew about it except me," Maria told us. "Even my cousins knew. And yet everyone hid it from me. It was a giant family conspiracy. How do you think that made me feel?"

Tanya's Story

"Finding out I was pregnant, having the boy I thought loved me walk out of my life without a word, having a baby at seventeen—it was the worst time in my whole life," Tanya said. "I put my little boy up for adoption because I knew it would be the best thing I could do for him. No one in my family has ever mentioned him or his birth since.

"I have been married for nineteen years now to a fellow I met in college, and he and I have three great kids. But my husband knows nothing about that long ago teenage fling and my illegitimate first child. I feel terrible about keeping such a thing from him, but after so much time has passed I can't just walk up and say, 'Guess what, dear. I have a son somewhere who is twenty-four years old.' Yet I live in daily fear that my first son will somehow search me out and will come knocking on my door."

Adoption Secrets

What are the secrets hidden by families who have adopted children or who have put children up for adoption? Here are some of the most common scenarios.

We Won't Tell

Sometimes there is a conscious decision on the part of the adoptive parents. They specifically decide to keep the truth from their child, and they caution all relatives or friends who know about it to keep their mouths shut. While other adoptive parents don't actually make this decision, they, like Claudia's parents, just never seem to get around to talking about it. Either way, it becomes a family secret.

I'm Your Mother

This secret occurs when a child is told that the wrong person is her mother (a grandmother, for instance, or an aunt).

That's Not What the Agency Said

There are some instances when an agency has been less than truthful with adoptive parents. One couple found out that their adolescent daughter was born to drug-addicted parents. The girl's adoptive mother discovered the truth by digging relentlessly to find an explanation for her daughter's learning disabilities.

"Why did you lie to us when we asked if her parents had been on drugs?" the girl's mother demanded of the agency worker.

The worker answered, "Because we were afraid you wouldn't take her if you knew the truth. We figured once you saw her and had a chance to bond with her, her background wouldn't matter to you."

We Don't Know Your Background

Sometimes adoptive parents are told about a child's background, but they don't like what they hear. So when the child begins to ask questions, the parents simply say, "Sorry, we don't know. No one told us anything."

This Adoption Isn't Working

One of the most painful situations that can occur in an adoption is when a child and the family just cannot make the adoption work, and the child has to be "returned." It doesn't happen often, and most of the failures involve children who were older and already set in their ways when they were adopted. But it is hardly possible to overestimate the damage that is done and the overwhelming feelings of failure experienced by everyone when such a failure does occur. The parents are consumed with guilt. The child, already convinced that he is a loser, gets yet another blow to his sense of self-worth. "I couldn't even do this right!" both sides tell themselves.

The secret occurs when the parents are not able to face and work through their sense of failure. Instead of facing the situation honestly, they lie to hide what has happened. One couple who made the decision to return the eight-year-old boy they had in their home for six months told their friends and relatives, "We wanted so much to keep Richie, but his mother came forward and wanted him back."

I Want to Find My Birth Parents

Probably the circumstance the majority of adoptive parents dread most is the possibility that their children may one day announce, "I want to find my birth mother." To keep this from happening, some parents make up unsavory backgrounds about their adopted children's birth parents. ("The woman you were born to is in prison.") Or they hide the information they have and say they know nothing that will help in the search. ("We would love to help you, but we don't have any information about your background.") Or they act so hurt and shocked that their children will feel guilty enough that they will never bring the subject up again.

Many parents rationalize their actions by saying, "Well, it's for my child's own good. If she finds her biological mother, she will just be disappointed and hurt."

Your Mother Was a Nice Person, But . . .

Because parents love their kids and want to protect them from pain, they can fall into the trap of keeping secret what they consider unsavory facts about the children's origins. Some parents feel it would harm their children to know they were born to unmarried women. They don't want them to know they were the products of rape or incest, or that one parent was gay or in prison, or that the child was taken away because of abuse or neglect. Some adoptive parents even hide the details of their children's ethnic background or the medical history of their birth families.

One mother gave this reason for not telling her son that his birth parents had been involved in the use and sale of drugs: "It will give the boy ideas. He'll follow right along in his father's footsteps." Other parents say the same thing about their children's illegitimate births. ("If she knows her mother got pregnant when she was only fourteen, our daughter will probably go out and do the same thing. Like mother, like daughter.")

Others say, "If he knew where he came from, it would strip away every bit of his self-esteem."

Your Dad Always Wanted a Boy

When one parent insists on adopting a child of a particular sex, other siblings—and even the other parent—can grow to resent it.

"Obviously, having four daughters made my father feel like a failure as a man," a young woman said with a touch of bitterness. "When my parents adopted a baby boy, my dad couldn't stop bragging about his new son. We girls just weren't good enough for him." The secret in this family was *Daughters are not as desirable as sons.*

You Were Born to Us

Today, children in our society who are living with both their biological parents are in the minority. Yet often times blended families want to hide the fact that their children have been adopted by their stepfathers (or sometimes by their stepmothers). "In all ways but biological, my husband is those children's father," one woman said of her second husband. "So why should I make a distinction to them? My children are better off thinking of him as their biological father."

It's All Because My Child Is Adopted

Many adoptive parents who have never raised a biological child look at everything that happens in their children's lives through adoption glasses. The child has a weight problem? "It's because she is adopted," they say. He's having trouble in school? "Well, you have to understand that he is adopted." Rebellious? "After all, the child *is* adopted."

The secret here is that, deep down, the parents believe that their child is inherently flawed. Subtly, the distinction is that the adoptive family is superior and the adopted child inferior. The Spiegle family is an example of this type of thinking.

The Spiegles were an enviable family. Mr. Spiegle was a successful and well paid CEO, and Mrs. Spiegle was the epitome of a fulfilled homemaker. Their older son and daughter, both born to the Spiegles, excelled at everything they tried. Their boy was a distinguished graduate of Annapolis, and their older daughter was in medical school on a full scholarship. Their youngest child, Rayleen, had been adopted as an infant.

Rayleen had the misfortune to be a normal child. All her life she was compared to her fast-paced, upward moving, success-oriented brother and sister. But try as she might, she never could manage to keep up with them. By the age of sixteen, Raylene had become totally out of hand, seemingly bent on embarrassing her family. One Sunday she and a group of her rowdy friends roared up on their motorcycles, parked at the church steps, and loudly played rock-and-roll music as the service ended and the worshipers left. Raylene thought this was especially funny.

Whenever Raylene's name came up, her family would shake their heads and say, "We should have known. She is adopted, after all."

Whether by birth or by adoption, children in a

family are different from one another. But the differences can be interesting. In one family where there were several biological children and one adopted child, the mother said, "Everyone is always telling me, 'Of all your children, Kara is the most like you.' Kara is our adopted child. Yet even I can see the similarities between us. Funny, isn't it?" Maybe, but not surprising. So much of what binds families together is what we learn from one another.

While it doesn't always make sense to tell a child every sordid detail of his background, especially when the child is young, few things can be as devastating to a child as finding out that his parents lied to him. "Parents are supposed to be honest with their kids," one boy explained. "If they lied to me about that, how can I believe *anything* they tell me? And how can I know there isn't a lot of important stuff they are hiding from me?"

Secret Letters

The letters that sometimes come to adoptive parents from biological parents can be confusing and threatening. These letters, generally written shortly after the baby's birth, are penned at a very difficult moment in the birth mother's life, often by a girl who is young and confused by many different stresses and emotions.

One adoptive couple said, "What are we to do?

That letter was written by a thirteen-year-old girl, and came with instructions that it be given to our child when he is twelve. (She probably thought that twelve was a ripe old age!) The letter is sealed, and the instructions say we should give it to him unopened, so we have no idea what is in there. What should do we? Are we morally obligated to follow that thirteen-year-old child's instructions?"

A tough dilemma indeed. But above all, the principle in operation is that the welfare of this child, is the responsibility of the adoptive parents. They owe nothing to the birth parents but everything to the child. We would strongly suggest that adoptive parents not give a child a sealed letter written by a birth parent in questionable emotional condition. Yet such a letter can easily become a secret, which is not helpful, either.

The best route is for adoptive parents to open any letter received and read it, regardless of the instructions. Only then will the parents be in a position to decide when and how to give it to the child. Decide on an appropriate age, and give the letter to the child then, telling him, "We wanted to be honest with you, but we also wanted to act responsibly. So we read the letter, and decided this is the right time for you to get it."

In the case of a letter arriving at some later time from a birth parent, it is perfectly appropriate for the adoptive parents to explain to the sender that they will not give the child a sealed letter but must have the opportunity to read it first. That way the parents are being honest with the sender as well as with the child.

The Costs of Adoption Secrets

However well-intentioned adoption secrets may be, they exact a high cost. Families who harbor adoption secrets foster:

- low self-esteem in their adopted children.
- feelings of loneliness and being unwanted.
- feelings of being different and feelings of isolation.
- feelings of being left out. This can especially happen when another child's efforts and accomplishments are not talked about for fear that her successes will undermine the adopted child. This is a sure way to cause resentment between children.
- shame on the part of adopted children who feel that the specifics of their background wouldn't be kept secret if they weren't bad.
- the perpetuation of lies and secrets. If it is okay for mother and father to stretch the truth and keep secrets, then surely it is okay for kids to do the same.

Healing Hints

There are specific steps to help a family move toward healing if adoption secrets have been harbored.

1. *Gather as many facts about adoption as possible.* This is something best done before the adoption takes place, to help prevent secrets from developing. But if that has not already been done, start now to

accumulate information. Read books and articles. Understand the emotional commitment an adoption involves. Become acquainted with the problems as well as the joys, the challenges as well as the blessings.

2. *Get as much information on your child as possible.* At the time of his adoption, ask for information on his background, his birth parents, their medical history, their talents and interests and abilities. Accept and save any pictures, letters, heirlooms, or whatever else is offered. If this has not been done, go back now and gather together anything available.

3. *Talk about the child's adoption openly among the members of the family.* Without dwelling on the subject or making a big deal of it, interject the word and concept of adoption as a comfortable and natural part of family life. ("Oh, yes, I remember Mr. Sorrell. We met him just before we adopted Aaron.") Talk about the adoption with the child, and answer her questions in a way that is appropriate to her age. ("Where were you born? In New York. That is a long, long way from here. It was just before Christmas that we flew back to get you.")

4. *Use ceremony in the life of the adopted child.* For some, this celebration may include the birth parents. Or it may be an acknowledgment of the date the child joined the family. One family had an

annual "adoption day" party for each of their children until they were ten years old. Similar to a birthday party, this annual event marked the importance of that date for the entire family.

5. *Be prepared for the possibility that the child will someday want to locate her birth parents.* You may even be willing to assist her in her search. Let her know you do not feel threatened by such a search. Let her know that nothing will change your love for her or her standing as your child.

Perhaps the most wonderful and exciting thing about adoption is that it is a way of building a family that was instituted and modeled by God Himself. As His adopted sons and daughters, all Christians are truly His children with all the rights and privileges that come with it. What a complete and perfect family relationship!

In his letter to the Galatians, the apostle Paul wrote: "But when the fullness of the time had come, God sent forth His Son, born of a woman, born under the law, to redeem those who were under the law, that we might receive the adoption as sons. And because you are sons, God has sent forth the Spirit of His Son into your hearts, crying out, 'Abba [Daddy], Father!' " (Gal. 4:4–6).

Could there be a more perfect example for adoptive parents? Could adoption be any more perfectly framed with truth and honesty?

10

Secrets of Grief and Loss

Thomas was used to being a very important person. As the manager of a large department of an international company, he was used to traveling first class, having a generous expense account, and having secretaries and assistants at his beck and call. Then came the unimaginable: Thomas's department was disbanded and he was out of work.

It wasn't Thomas who came in for counseling. It was his wife, Christine. "I'm at the end of my rope," she said. "I can understand my husband's range of feelings, I really can. Sometimes it is rage, sometimes self-pity, sometimes shame, sometimes fear, and always uncertainty. But the thing is, he steadfastly refuses to accept any help or support. He has shut himself off from everybody—his family and his friends. Thomas's secret feeling was *Success makes me important, and working is a part of success.*

"Thomas won't do anything to get help for himself. He keeps insisting he's fine, that he's just getting the break he's been needing from his busy schedule. He says that after he's rested up, everything will be like it used to be."

Because of his inability to handle the loss of his job, Thomas is passing a message on to his children: "It is not okay to suffer loss. If you do, you are a failure."

Types of Losses

We tend to think of losses in terms of death. While this certainly is an important loss, losses also come in many other forms, with their own unique set of issues for families. And unless we have a very short or extraordinary life, we will eventually suffer several kinds of loss.

Financial Loss

Such a loss may involve an actual loss of money—sometimes a great deal of money—but it can also involve the loss of a job, the loss of a business, or even the loss of one's financial status.

As with Thomas, the family secret becomes one of failure. Not only is the loss itself painful, even devastating, it batters one's sense of self-worth.

Family secret: *Financial loss equals failure.*

Loss of a Potential Family

Many people who never marry experience a profound sense of loss. The same is true of many who never have children.

At forty-one, Victoria is still single. Even her mother has stopped asking her if she is ever going to get married and give her grandchildren. Although almost everyone she knows is or has been married and has children, Victoria doesn't talk about her singleness with anyone. She needs to grieve the loss of not being married, but how can she when neither she nor anyone else ever mentions it?

Family secret: *Single people are not complete.*

Manuel and Loretta Delgado suffered a different kind of loss. Married nine years, they have never been able to have a child. Loretta put it this way: "Every day of my life, I carry in my heart the pain of the child who might have been." Yet she and Manuel do not talk about this child who never was. "I know we should dwell on the positive," Loretta said. "We should be thankful for all we do have. So I always try to keep a happy thought and a smile on my face." Manuel and Loretta have never grieved their loss. How can something as obvious as not being married or not having children become a secret? The secret is the unspoken pain.

Family secret: *Those who are childless are not complete.*

Loss of Significant Relationships

This includes such losses as family estrangements, divorce, desertion, and even the loss of close friends.

When they were growing up, sisters Virginia and Helene enjoyed a close relationship. But two years ago, there was a serious misunderstanding between them, and the two haven't spoken to each other since.

What does the rest of the family say? No one knows. Both Helene and Virginia refuse to talk about the disagreement with anyone.

Family secret: *Never say you are sorry.*

Divorce is an especially difficult loss to deal with openly and honestly, for usually it is steeped in deception, anger, and defensiveness. Many times there is also a good bit of cover-up going on.

When Sharon's husband left her for someone else, she couldn't deal with the deep hurt and betrayal. All she told her five-year-old daughter, Amy, was, "Daddy went away." Even at her tender age, Amy knew better than to press her mom for details. Yet she grew up wondering where her Daddy was, and she always thought that if she was a really good little girl, Daddy would come home again.

But Daddy never did come home, and today Amy is struggling with her distrust of men. She still wonders what she did back then that drove her father away.

Family secret: *It's all my fault. Men can't be trusted.*

Fifty-year-old Glenda has always told everyone— even her own children—that her father died when she was very young. But the truth is that Glenda's father deserted his wife and family. "I don't even know whether or not he is still alive," Glenda admitted in private. She has all kinds of unresolved feelings about him, yet she cannot share her pain. The subject is taboo for the entire family.

Family secret: *There is no reason to talk about something you can't change.*

Emily does not understand how to deal appropriately with changes in her relationships with people. When her husband got a job transfer, the family had to move away from the small town where she had grown up. Emily was devastated.

When her daughter, Jamie, complained that she didn't have any friends, Emily said, "I knew everyone in my high school. Something is wrong here." When Jamie failed to get a part in the school play, Emily stormed down to the school and accused the director of discriminating against her daughter. When Jamie didn't get into all the classes she wanted, Emily stormed down to the principal's office to protest. Jamie begged her mom to stay home, but Emily said, "I should get to know him anyway. My mother always knew the people at my school and we never had any trouble getting what we wanted."

"I hate my new school," Jamie said. "If it was a good school, I would know the other kids by now. I wish it was special and close like my mom's high school was."

Family secret: *Nothing is as good as it was back then. If relationships with people change, it isn't right.*

Loss of Youth

It is a strange statement on the priorities of our society that so many of us harbor a deep fear of losing our youth. Although we concede that it is inevitable, and that it happens to everyone sooner or later, we don't see anything positive about getting older.

As Grady approaches his sixtieth birthday, he is more and more aware that he is slowing down. "I'm getting old, and it scares me," he thinks. But instead of sharing his fears with his wife and planning how they want to spend their future years, Grady broods alone. His children would like to talk to their parents about retirement plans, but they don't dare. Grady has let them know it is too sensitive a subject to be broached.

Family secret: *Don't talk about anything that may upset someone.*

Losses of Illness and Death

Few losses leave people as confused and unable to communicate as serious illness and death. No one seems to know what to say to anyone else.

When Dirk was killed in a car accident, his death was so sudden and so cripplingly painful, that his family stopped talking about him altogether. His belongings were bundled up and stored in the garage, and all his pictures taken down and put away. It was almost as though Dirk had never been a part of the family.

It's not that Dirk's family hadn't loved him. On the contrary, they had loved him so dearly that rather than confront their pain, they chose to ignore reality. But because they were not able to talk about their father, Dirk's children couldn't begin to grieve his death.

Family secret: *If we don't talk about it, we don't have to feel the pain.*

Death losses carry on to the next generation when the children say, "We never got to say goodbye." It leaves a lot of unfinished business, and the pain carries over into other relationships. Often people who have suffered loss don't allow themselves to get close to other people. It is a protective wall they build up around themselves. They cannot handle the idea of ever being in a position to be so badly hurt again.

Keeping quiet closes down the healthy grieving process. It actually prevents healing from taking place. This is particularly evident when talking about an impending death.

Wesley was eighty years old and in the last excruciating stage of cancer. He knew his life was coming to an end, and he desperately wanted to talk to his family about what was happening to him. He wanted to share his fears and worries and hopes and last wishes with the people who were dearest to him. For one thing, Wesley was terrified that he would be put onto a life-support system. He longed for assurance that he would be given enough medication to keep him from suffering too much pain, and then allowed to leave this life in peace. Most of all, Wesley wanted to say good-bye to his family, and to tell his son how sorry he was about the strife that had gone on between them for so many years.

Wesley never got to say any of those things. Every time he tried to talk about his approaching death, his family cut him off. "You're going to be okay," they would say cheerily. "You're going to live for a long,

long time." Or, "We will talk about all that later. Now you just get a good rest."

The last weeks of Wesley's life could have been a time of healthy grieving and healing, but they were not. Wesley's family couldn't let him say good-bye.

Family secret: *If we pretend it won't happen, maybe it won't.*

Loss by Suicide

Suicide is probably the most difficult of all deaths to talk about. Many families choose to say nothing at all. Others lie.

Barry was nineteen years old when he shot himself in the head with his father's hunting rifle. Even though Barry's death was ruled a suicide, his devastated parents, sister, and grandparents maintained that it had been a hunting accident.

Barry's family couldn't cope with the guilt they felt about not having seen the signs of his despair. Each person was consumed with the certainty that he or she should have been able to stop him. Instead of admitting to and dealing with their anger at Barry's actions, and rather than confronting the terrible anguish that suicide inevitably brings, the family projected their rage onto the doctor and the coroner who had dared to rule the young man's death a suicide.

Family secret: *If you blame someone else, then you won't have to deal with your own feelings.*

Why the Secrets?

As with other areas of family secrets, there is always the question, Why are the losses kept secret? Certainly any grief is painful, but why not acknowledge it as such? Why allow it to grow into a family secret? Once again, the reasons are directly related to the deepest negative human emotions: fear, shame, and insecurity.

Fear

Family secrets arise when there is the fear that family members, or others who are grieving, simply cannot handle the pain. Many people panic when someone they love cries, is hurting deeply, or disappears in death. They can't fix it, they can't make it better, they can't lessen the pain. So they avoid the grief, and it becomes a secret.

Other people fear that in their grief they will break down or fall apart in front of others. They fear losing control or being pitied. Yet that "breaking down" is the very beginning of healing.

Shame

People view some losses with shame, humiliation, and embarrassment because they somehow feel that it means they themselves are failures, that the loss was their fault. This unfair and unnecessary burden creates family secrets.

Insecurity

Secrets also grow out of insecurity that causes a person to feel she might lose whatever she has left as well. When a person is dying, for instance, those close to that person may feel that they are not going to be able to make it through the sorrow. Life will be changed. "If I lose this person," they feel, "nothing in my life will ever be the same."

After a neighborhood in southern California was destroyed by fire, the neighbors began to meet to talk about their losses and to discuss ways of coping. Three years later, some people are still getting together regularly. Only now they meet in their lovely, rebuilt homes. "But the thing is, it's just not the same," one woman explained. "It's not the same house with the same things in it. It will *never* be the same."

People crippled by insecurity are unable to get through the grieving process because they're stuck right there in it. They are unable to admit that something terrible did happen—but now they need to go on.

The Cost of Keeping Grief and Loss Secrets

A loss that is not talked about and never grieved does not go away. The person just keeps on carrying the loss around, piling it on top of other unresolved griefs, until he accumulates so many losses and so much pain that he is forced to deal with them.

Some people have never been taught to grieve. Instead, they have been taught to stuff in their feelings and be careful never to let them pop out. After doing this again and again and again, something relatively small, such as a job loss, can send such a person into a terrible depression. It's not the final loss that does it. It's the pressure of all those other accumulated losses.

And there is a definite cost to keeping secrets. People who harbor such secrets:

- suffer from a loss of intimacy and support from others.
- lose their sense of self-worth and respect.
- have a great deal of difficulty making sound decisions.
- can become suicidal.
- are unable to trust.
- blame themselves for whatever has happened, and feel responsible for things for which they in no way bear a responsibility.
- are unable to deal with the emotional realities of their lives. The secrets are a major trigger of addictive behaviors that are themselves passed along to the next generation.

Years ago, when Leah was eight years old, her father killed himself. No one ever talked about the suicide. The whole thing was much too shameful. To make matters worse, Leah and her mother were plunged into poverty by her father's death. Her mother was so embittered, she rarely mentioned the name of Leah's father.

At a very early age, Leah learned that men are selfish and cannot be trusted. She well remembered that when she needed her father most, he bailed out and left her mother and her to fend for themselves.

Leah did marry, and she had a son and a daughter of her own. Leah loved her family, but she kept a great emotional distance from her husband, and both she and her husband remained at arm's length from their children. In high school her son began to use drugs, although Leah had no idea there was a problem until the teenager died from an overdose. His friends said he had talked a lot about killing himself. They were convinced it was suicide, not an accident.

Leah's daughter, Donna, was absolutely devastated by her brother's death. And she was hurt and puzzled at her mother's refusal to talk about him or even mention his name.

When Donna married and had a son, she named the baby after her brother. Donna was so overly protective of her son that she began to drive her husband away. Eventually even her son began to pull away from her. It was at her husband's insistence that the troubled family finally began therapy.

"It seems our whole family history is one of sadness and pain," Donna said. "I just can't understand it."

Only as they began to chip away at the secrets and expose the hidden pain that had moved through the generations did the family begin to understand. "Everyone I love dies," Donna said miserably. "My brother was the closest person in my life. How could he have left me?"

The pain of ungrieved suicides had first left Leah, then Donna, fearful that they would lose others they loved.

The family's story has a happy ending. By working through her grief, Donna was able to loosen her grip on her son in a healthy way. And as the family began to heal, Donna persuaded her mom to come along with them to their family counseling sessions.

"To think, it all started with my father's suicide," Leah said recently. "Who would have thought so much pain and suffering could come from a loss ungrieved?"

Healing Hints

All losses need to be grieved. It doesn't matter whether the people around you consider your loss large or small, important or trivial, valid or invalid. It isn't their loss; it's yours, and it needs to be grieved. One problem is that people recognize the need to grieve tangible losses much more readily than they understand the need to grieve intangible losses.

Tangible losses are those things you can see, touch, and experience. Facing your own death or the death of a loved one is a tangible loss. So is losing a job or going through a divorce. (Not all tangible losses are as huge as these. A lost possession, a scratched car, a friend who moves away, a pet that dies—these, too, are all tangible losses.)

Intangible losses are more illusive: the baby you never had, the nurturing parent you always longed for, the ideal mate who is not to be yours, the happy childhood you missed, the goal you now know you will never reach. These are intangible losses, the ones people so often tell you to "quit dwelling on." But these losses, too, need to be grieved.

Here are some hints to help those who are grieving.

1. *Refuse to repress grief.* Understand that there is no virtue in "being strong." Don't be afraid to mourn and cry.

2. *Grief is a process*, first outlined by Elisabeth Kübler-Ross, in her book *On Death and Dying* (New York: MacMillan, 1969). When you are going through the process and experiencing the pain, it will seem that it will never end. You will think you are never going to get better. When this despair overtakes you, remember that there are different stages to grief—all crucial to healing. Understand that by feeling the pain, you know you are in the process of healing. Soak yourself in God's promises, and trust His faithfulness over the feelings of the moment.

3. *Don't minimize the pain.* Refuse to compare your suffering to someone else's, and don't allow anyone else to compare theirs with yours. When you are suffering, your pain will seem almost unbearable. Validate your pain by refusing comparisons.

4. *Tell the story over and over and over again.* The telling and retelling is a part of the healing process. But as you may have already discovered, even your most faithful friends and dearest loved ones get tired of hearing those retellings. So widen your network. Join a support group where you can all listen to each other's stories, and where you will learn that you truly are not alone. Easy answers are not what you need. A listening ear is.

5. *Give yourself a break from the grief.* Grief comes and it goes. Allow yourself to laugh and enjoy life when you can. Do something that will take your mind off your grief for a while. This is something children do naturally. Their mom dies, and the next day they are out in the yard playing and laughing. Adults see them and think, "How can those children be so happy? Didn't they care about their mother?" A break in the grief is a God-given natural mechanism, one most adults seem to bypass.

6. *Give yourself time to heal.* Sometimes, when we are hurting, the Christian community especially tries to push us to look at others instead of at ourselves. Mistakenly, they see self-absorption as a sign of selfishness. If you doubt that it is indeed all right to grieve, look at the example Jesus set for us. In Matthew 26:36–44, we read about Jesus' excruciating prayer in the garden. He said, "My soul is exceedingly sorrowful, even to death. Stay here and watch with Me" (v. 38). If Jesus was sorrowful unto

death, what makes you think you have to be happy and positive and brave?

Because we are human beings living in an imperfect world, we *will* experience loss and grief. It is an inescapable part of life. When you encounter those dark days, you will be faced with a significant decision: How will you allow the pain of the present to affect your future? Will you allow bitterness or denial to separate you from God? Or will you choose to draw close to Him, to feel His strength and love, and to let Him heal your hurts? He promises,

> Fear not, for I have redeemed you; I have called you by your name; you are Mine. When you pass through the waters, I will be with you; and through the rivers, they shall not overflow you. When you walk through the fire, you shall not be burned, nor shall the flame scorch you. For I am the LORD your God, the Holy One of Israel, your Savior" (Isa. 43:1–3).

Grieve, be comforted, and move on toward healing.

11

Beyond the Secrets: Becoming Healthy

Angela grew up in a family steeped in secrets. Her father was abusive, both physically and sexually. Her mother seemed passive and distant, yet she fought back in her own way—with wild spending sprees that periodically plunged the family into financial turmoil. Angela's brother, Lloyd, had been addicted to drugs since he was nineteen. Just released from prison where he served a five-year term for armed robbery, thirty-two-year-old Lloyd is once again living with his parents. Angela herself has struggled since her high school days with eating disorders. Her sister Diana, twenty-eight, has been married twice and is now involved in what she calls a "live-in relationship."

"I know we have problems," Angela said. "We're a messed-up family. I always knew it, but what can you do? Your family is your family, good, bad or indifferent. Can anything ever really change?"

Chapter 2 noted that healing begins when one person in a family steps forward and breaks the secrecy. For when one person identifies, acknowledges, and tells a family secret, the action gives permission to others in the family to bring their secrets out into the open.

Angela was the one who took that first step in her family. "For the umpteenth time I had gone looking for treatment for my wild eating binges," she said. "But for the first time I came away with more than a notebook full of diets and recipes and memories of rousing inspirational speeches. This time I had a challenge. 'What's really eating at you?' the counselor had asked me. 'Let's get at the root of your problem and attack it there.' "

Angela knew what was eating her. It was her family and all the sham and hypocrisy she saw there. Although every member of her family knew about the problems, no one ever addressed them. For instance, her parents always referred to Lloyd's time in prison as "when he was out of town."

"I wanted to scream, 'What's the matter with all of you? Lloyd wasn't on vacation! He was in a federal penitentiary!'" Angela said. "But instead I did exactly what everyone else did. I ignored his tattooed hand, his swagger, and his surly attitude, and pretended my brother was just back from a long fishing trip."

But then Angela determined to stand up to her family's secrets. She paid her parents a two-day visit and told them, "I am in counseling, trying to work through the nightmares I still have about the things you did to me, Dad, and the help I never got from you, Mom."

Angela's hope was that breaking the secrecy would open her parents' eyes. "I wanted them to think, *Look what we've done because of this secret, and we never dealt with it. Let's deal with it right now.*"

"It didn't happen," Angela reported. "They just stared at me for a minute, and then my father got up and stomped out of the room, slamming the door behind him. My mother smiled and said, 'Well, I think I'll go in and make an apple crunch pie for dinner. I know it's your favorite.' "

Angela had admitted the problem. But with her first step she immediately ran into a brick wall—her family's denial. What to do now?

Make a Plan for Healing

Healing doesn't just happen. It requires a plan of attack. Some of the specific issues here have been addressed already at the end of previous chapters in the "Healing Hints."

Even so, there are several basic principles that apply in every type of family secret.

Take Responsibility for Yourself

Angela was on the right track, for she had already told herself, "I am hurting." And she followed up this recognition with the decision, "I am not willing to keep on hurting." Now she was coming to terms with the truth about herself. She was beginning a walk back through her life-long emotional pain. But a family works something like a machine. Healthy or not, it has a set functioning pattern, and so long as all members play their parts, it keeps on going around and around and around. But when someone steps out of the line—breaks the family secret—it's as if a wrench has been thrown into the machine. Chaos sets in, and the family can no longer function.

These changes do not come easy. Sometimes it happens that things get a whole lot worse before they get better. For when things suddenly no longer work the way they always did, it can make for an exceedingly uncomfortable situation. There may even be a total loss of some relationships. In Angela's case, her parents' refusal to admit to secret-keeping meant the relationship was severed. But her sister Diana immediately called her and said she was glad Angela had spoken up.

Through many long talks and open sharing with each other, Angela and Diana learned to give and receive love for the first time.

Understand the Lies and Accept the Truth

Lies keep people trapped and block healing. Root out those lies and search out what is true. Prayer, Scripture reading, and wise counsel will help to make those distinctions.

A good way to understand the lies is to figure out how the secret started in the first place. Where are the weaknesses in the family that led to accepting the lie as truth? Where is your own weak spot?

"My father always told me God gave him the right to rule over our family just as Christ ruled over the church," Angela said. "It sounds silly now, but I actually defended my father because he used Scripture to prove his point. It wasn't until my minister told me that God fully intends us to use our common sense, and that we are not to take phrases and verses out of context, that I even dared question my father."

When Angela understood the lie, she was able to confront it with truth.

Mend Your Relationship with God

In 1 John 1:5–7 we read:

> This is the message which we have heard from Him and declare to you, that God is light and in Him is no darkness at all. If we say that we have fellowship with Him, and walk in darkness, we lie and do not practice the truth. But if we walk in the light as He is in the light, we have fellowship with one another, and the blood of Jesus Christ His Son cleanses us from all sin.

If you have begun to move away from the secrets and the lies they spawn and seek out the truth, you have already begun to mend your relationship with God. Now be totally honest with God about yourself. Confess any part you had in starting or in keeping the secret. Christ promises that "If we confess our sins, He is faithful and just to forgive us our sins and to cleanse us from all unrighteousness" (1 John 1:9). Claim this promise and receive forgiveness from God.

Mend Your Relationship with Yourself

Once a person has consciously accepted the forgiveness God offers, and the healing Jesus Christ provides, it is possible to build a healthy self-esteem by
setting boundaries in your life which glorify God. See
yourself as you really are, with no pretense to be perfect or to keep up appearances. This will allow you to
take off that old mask and reveal the real you under-
neath. Ask God to empower you to stop playing the
old roles of the past. Review the "Helpful Hints" in
previous chapters for the specific issues your own secret
involves.

Mend Your Relationship with Others

Who are the people with whom there are relationships in need of mending? Parents? Siblings? Spouse?
Children? Begin by sharing with these people honestly
and lovingly. Admit your own faults. Talk about the
secrets without accusations or judgment. The apostle
James tell us: "Confess your trespasses to one another,
and pray for one another, that you may be healed. The
effective, fervent prayer of a righteous man avails
much" (James 5:16).

Give the others a chance to talk as well, and when
they do talk, listen without interrupting. If their version
of what happened is different than yours, don't be too
quick to tell them they are wrong. Remember that even
your memories may be colored by your feelings and
perceptions.

Offer and accept forgiveness. This may be terribly, terribly hard, but as you struggle, remember that God has established the pattern for forgiveness by offering to forgive you for anything you have ever done or ever will do. Anything!

Whether or not you are able to achieve mended relationships, it is important to assume as much a manner of mutual respect as possible. Being able to show respect is a mark of healing. But that's not to say there should be no boundaries set. There should be, for both sides. Respect doesn't mean you have to like or approve of everything that other person says and does. But whether that other person is right or wrong is his problem. Release your expectations and let it go.

One of the hardest things to achieve is learning to trust again. That will take effort and patience and plenty of time. For those who will come along, there can be a whole new relationship that was never there before. "Diana and I see a really close, loving relationship in our future," Angela said. "While my prospect with my mother is not so glowing, I do see a relationship of mutual respect between us. I know there are many things we will never really be able to discuss, but I see a lot more closeness than I ever would have thought possible."

Benchmarks of Increasing Health

With all the positives, "Sometimes I get discouraged," Angela admits. "I wonder if I really am getting any better after all. I can't trust my feelings. Is there some way I can know I am still improving?"

Angela is right about feelings. If you put too much faith in them, you will feel as though you are constantly riding a roller coaster. One day you may be at the top of the world, but the next you may plummet to the depths of the sea. Instead of trusting your feelings, look for the following benchmarks of health.

You are approaching emotional health if you . . .

- have quit trying to fix your family. Have you come to the point where you can honestly say, "I cannot change my family, but I can change myself"?
- are stopping the pain from going any farther. As you become more healthy, you will be able to prevent your children from being caught up in the malignant cycle of secrets.
- have been freed by the truth. John 8:32 says "And you shall know the truth, and the truth shall make you free." Are you moving toward joy, as your life is based more and more on truth and realness?
- are able to speak the truth in love. If there is a hurtful truth that needs to be confronted, is your own heart right and at peace so that you can share it lovingly?
- have confronted your fears. You are well on your

way to achieving health when your old fears are no longer able to catch up with you and hold you prisoner.

- are able to admit and accept your weaknesses. Healthy people are able to admit to their weaknesses, but do not let their weaknesses (such as inappropriate anger) control them.
- recognize your strengths. Healthy people have enough sense of reality and equilibrium to admit their strengths.
- are able to wait patiently for the final healing. Healthy people see time as their friend. They understand that patience is indeed a virtue. They look back and, rejoicing at how far they have come, recognize that they didn't make it this far overnight.

Hope for the Future

Scripture tells us that without a vision, the people perish. Having a new vision yourself, with realistic goals to aim toward, is the overarching theme that shows that healing is taking place.

Angela, who grew up surrounded by secrets, is no longer bound by them. Because the secrets are broken, because her past has been confronted, because the consequences have been dealt with, she has every confidence that the pain will stop in her generation.

"I can't say everything is fine and dandy now," Angela said. "But I can say this: From here on out, I have a fighting chance at a normal life. My children have better than that. And when my grandchildren come along, I have every confidence that they will be able to lead healthy, honest lives."

The same can be true for any family who has been keeping secrets—no matter for how many generations. It is only a matter of getting started.